PLAY BETTER CHESS TODAY!

A QUICK GUIDE TO IMPROVING YOUR CHESS!

ROSALYN B. KATZ
&
DAVID LAWRENCE KATZ

CARDOZA PUBLISHING

Dedicated to Charles Joseph Pole

Production and Design: Steven Marshall Katz
Many thanks to: Alan Stern, Charles Joseph Pole, Maurice Smith, and Troy Farrow for their help and support. Thanks also to the many young people in our pilot group, who gave us such good ideas and great feedback.

Library of Congress Catalog No: 2011933348
ISBN: 10: 1-58042-287-X
ISBN: 13 978-1-58042-287-1

Cardoza Publishing is the foremost gaming publisher in the world with a library of more than 200 up-to-date and easy-to-read books and strategies. These authoritative works are written by the top experts in their fields and with more than 10,000,000 books in print, represent the most popular gaming books anywhere.

Visit our website or write us for a full list of our books, software and advanced strategies.

CARDOZA PUBLISHING
P.O. Box 98115, Las Vegas, NV 89193
Phone (800)577-WINS
email: cardozabooks@aol.com
www.cardozabooks.com

TABLE OF CONTENTS

FOREWORD

Play Better Chess Today! was written for kids like you, who play chess and love the game. This book will give you ideas for winning, not just moving the pieces.

You'll learn to analyze — that is, figure out what moves you can make to improve your position. All during the game, there will be choices to make, and you will have control over what happens.

Playing chess is fun. Winning at chess is ... just great! Roz Katz and her son David Katz are just the ones to teach you how to win at chess. I've known them both for a very long time as chess players and as people. I most admire Roz for her work in the chess world and the fun she is to be around, and David is a USCF Life Master who used to live up here in Toronto. We really miss him at the Scarborough Chess Club. I don't know anyone better to author a book for children on the basic elements of improving chess skills.

Maurice Smith,
President, Canadian Chess Federation

A very active tournament director, teacher and chess player, Maurice Smith has for many years been a major force in the chess world. He's known, loved and respected internationally.

INTRODUCTION

Our cat plays the piano! Actually, she walks across the keys and makes noise! You want to play chess better than our cat plays piano. This book was written so that you will play chess better than our cat plays the piano.

For this book to work best for you, you need to know how to:

- ♔ Move, the pieces
- ♔ Check, mate, and draw
- ♔ Read and write your games

These basics of chess are in our first book, *Start Playing Chess Today!* If you already know the rules and basics of chess, this book will help you to play chess better — and have more fun.

Instead of hitting "wrong notes," making moves that lose your pieces, you will make beautiful moves ... and have a terrific time doing it!

Have fun with this book.

Tip: Have your chess set right near you as you read through this book. Then you can move the pieces on the board as you go over the games.

I. PIECES AND PAWNS

Chess play is teamwork, and each piece has its own job to do on the team. Look at the chess pieces and the pawn and see how their moves are different and special.

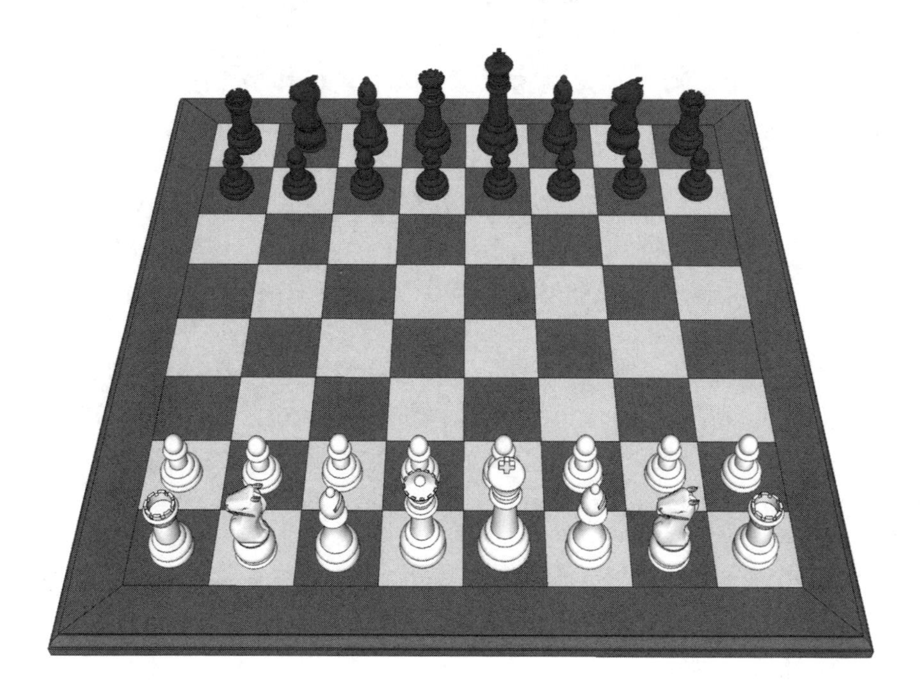

The Knight - N

The knight (**N**) move is a jump — two squares one way and one square at right angles (or L shape).

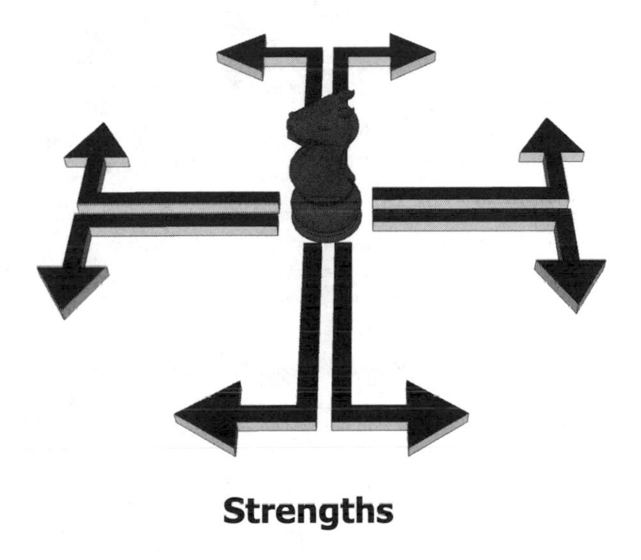

Strengths

The **N** moves differently from any other piece. It is good in closed positions on the board — when pawns and other pieces are in the way — because it can jump over them. It is the only chess piece that jumps. It is also the only piece that moves in a pattern instead of in a straight line.

Weaknesses

Because of the way it moves, the **N** is slow at moving across the board. It covers only certain squares in a large circle around it, so it needs to be in the middle of things. Look here.

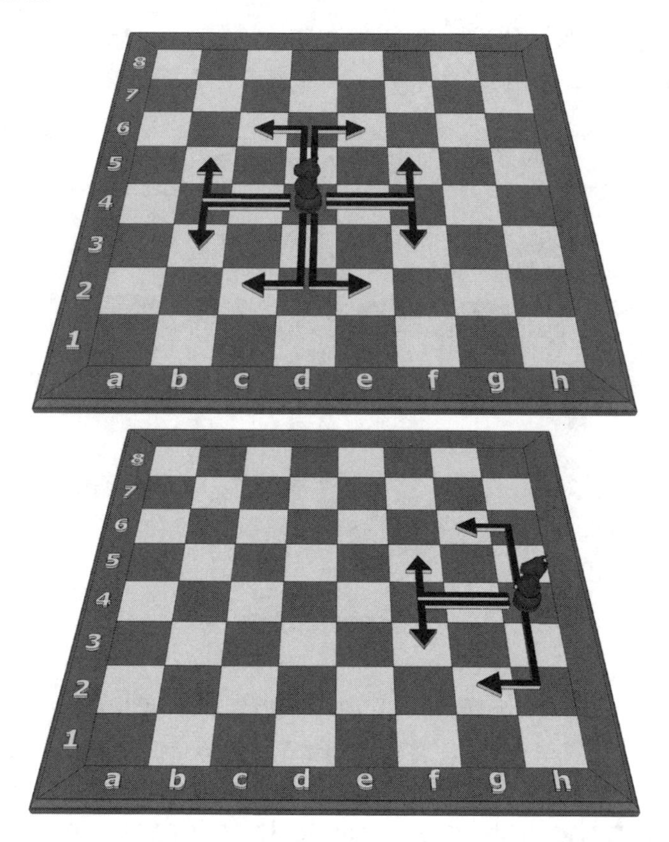

Can you see why it is not good for a **N** to be on the a or h file, at the sides of the board? The **N** controls 8 squares when it is on d4, but only 4 squares on h4.

Where would you rather have your **N?**

Each piece has a different job and moves differently.

The Rook - R

The rook (**R**) moves straight ahead in one direction as many squares as it needs.

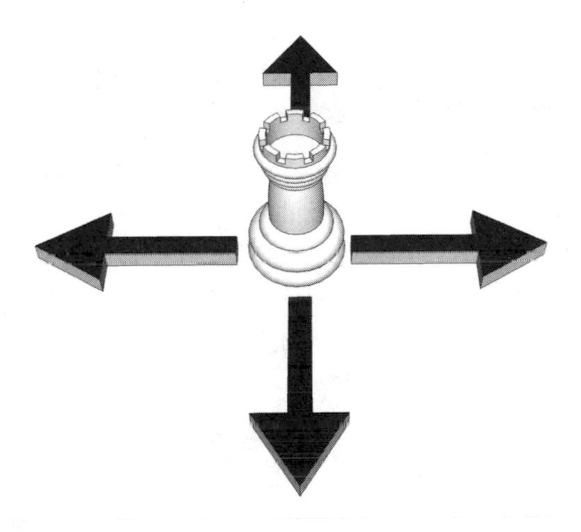

Strengths

The **R** moves fast when there is nothing in the way. It is a good piece to have when the board's ranks and files are mostly empty — open position.

Weaknesses

The **R** is not a good piece in closed positions — when its way is blocked by a lot of other pieces.

Look at the **R**s on this board. Which **R** is placed better? When you are deciding where to move your **R** remember that **R**s are better on open ranks and files.

The Bishop - B

The bishop (**B**) moves in one direction, diagonally, as far as it needs to.

Strengths

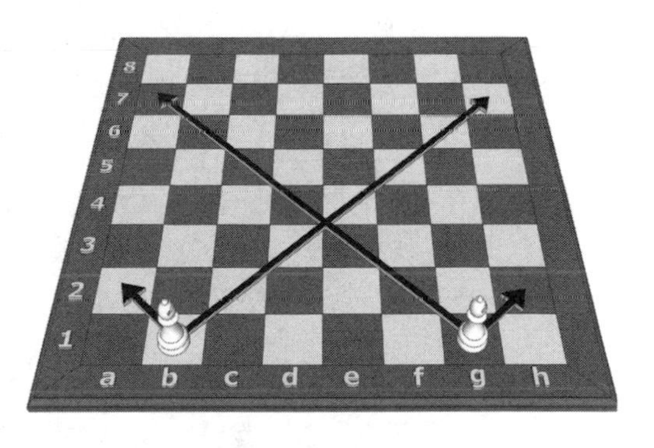

The **B** can move fast and far diagonally. When you have both your **B**s, they are very strong because they can work as a team: one covers black squares and one covers white squares. Their power is really cut when you have only one **B**.

Weaknesses

A **B** needs long, open diagonals in its color.

In a closed position, the **B** can be blocked by its own pawns.

Each **B** can move on only half of the board squares, white or black. It stays on the color square where it started.

The Queen - Q

The queen (**Q**) can move in any direction, as far as she wants to go, as long as nothing is in the way.

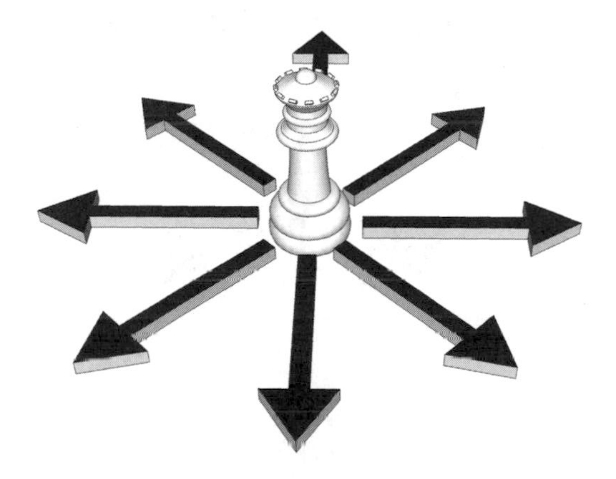

Strengths

The **Q** is the most powerful piece on the board. She combines the strengths of both **R** and **B**. She can move fast and in any direction. On the board, the **Q** controls more squares than any other piece.

Weaknesses

The **Q** can be "chased" by weaker pieces. Try not to move the **Q** out too early in the game. Your other pieces should come out first. It is good to have your queen active in any position, open or closed.

The pawn - a,b,c,d,e,f,g,h

Each pawn moves forward only one square at a time. It can move two squares forward, but only on its opening move. It moves diagonally to capture.

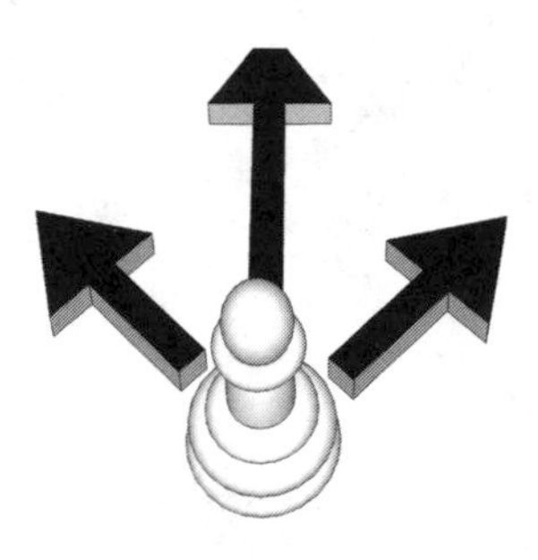

Strengths

The pawn, by crossing the board, can become a **Q** or any other piece. It can be used to defend other pieces.

Weaknesses

Once a pawn moves forward, it can't go back.
A pawn can be attacked or blocked easily.

The pawn moves only in one direction, forward, unless it is capturing. But remember the "en passant", "in passing" move? It goes like this...

♔ A pawn, on its first move, advances two squares

♔ It lands next to an enemy pawn (so that they're side by side).

♔ The enemy can capture that pawn as if it had moved only one square.

♔ This must happen right away, the enemy's next move must be the capture. Otherwise, forget about it, it's too late.

Here, the Black **d**-pawn captures the White **c**-pawn on c3.

You pretend "**c**" only moved one square!

The King - K

♚

The king (**K**) can move in any direction, but only one square at a time.

Strengths

Most important, if you still have your **K**, you know you haven't lost! The **K** can move in any direction. The **K** can castle. The **K** is the most help in the endgame and in closed positions. You always want to keep him safe, but remember that the **K** is a fighting piece — it can capture other pieces.

Weaknesses

The King needs to be protected all the time. It can't move fast enough to run from danger. The **K** is in most danger in open positions, from pieces that can move far and fast. Keep other pieces nearby to protect him.

II. POSITIONS

Chess games are made up of positions. White and black pieces move back and forth over the field of play, while pawns just try to get to the other side.

At the beginning of the game, both players move their pawns forward, toward each other, to let their other pieces out. The center of the board can become a pretty busy place. As pawns and pieces are captured, there is more room for the pieces left on the board to move.

Closed Position

Here is a closed position. You can see that all of the pawns are "stuck." Since they can only move forward, they get in the way of the other pieces.

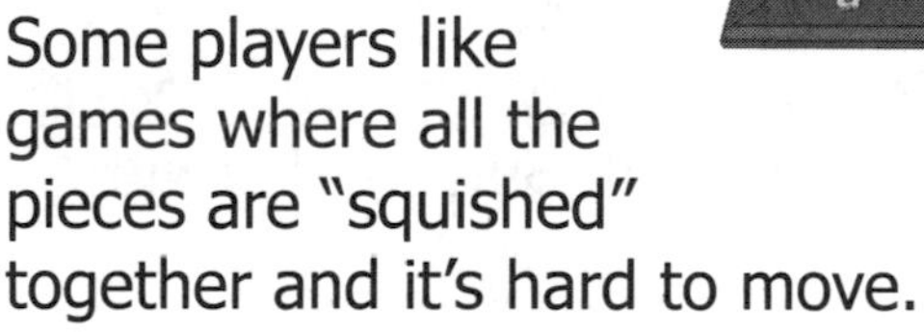

Some players like games where all the pieces are "squished" together and it's hard to move.

Closed Position Stars

Ns and **K**s are at their best in closed positions.

The **N** can jump over the other pieces, so it doesn't matter if something is in the way. Also, since a **N** can jump only to certain squares, it doesn't need tons of space around it in order to move, the way other pieces do. Watch out for the **N** on a closed position board!

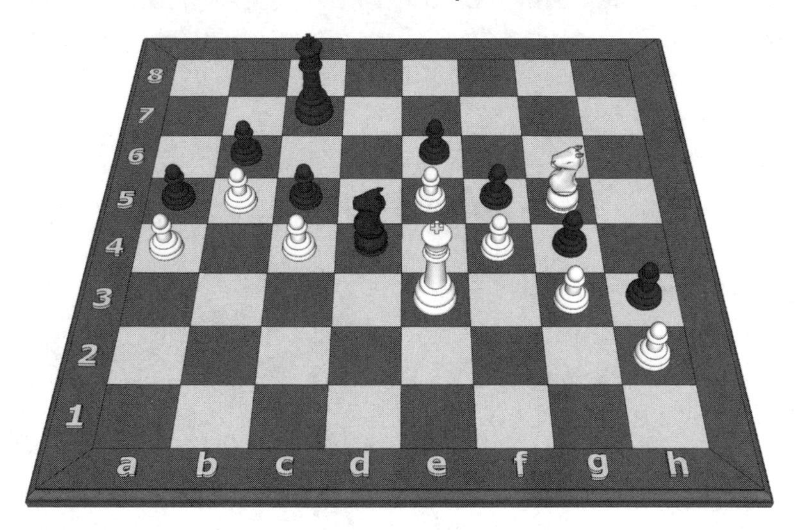

The **K** only moves one square at a time in any direction, so it doesn't need lots of open space. it is the prime target of the opposing pieces so open space is a danger. Make sure your **K** is always protected. Surround it with defenders.

In a closed position, if an enemy piece gets too close, don't forget that the **K** can also capture!

Open Position

This board shows an open position. With spaces between and in front of pawns, they are free to move forward and to trade.

Trade means you take an opponent's pawn diagonally, and your opponent diagonally takes one of yours. On an open board, your other pieces can make big moves, racing here and there across the board. Things can get pretty wild.

Sometimes you may play fast, open games. Other times your pawns will be locked with the other player's pawns in a closed position, unable to move. In some games, there aren't any pawns left on the board at all!

When you play, which kind of position is the most fun for you?

Open Position Stars

Bs, **R**s and **Q**s are at their best in open positions — they can really use the space and freedom to travel around the board.

Bs can move as far as you want them to diagonally. **R**s can move as far as you want them to across or up and down the board. The **Q** can move as far as you want her to, either up, down, and across the board or diagonally.

Beware of the **Q** in an open position game!

Cool Moves

Some moves just make you want to smile ... as long as your pieces aren't the ones in danger.

You look at the board. You suddenly see a move you can make that will attack two pieces at once even better, two important pieces at once! There comes that smile. You can't help but capture one of the two pieces on the play. These kinds of moves definitely add to the fun of chess.

The Fork

A "fork" in chess is when you are able to attack two pieces at the same time with only one of your pieces.

On this board, where should the white **N** go to fork the black pieces?

If you said d6, you got it!

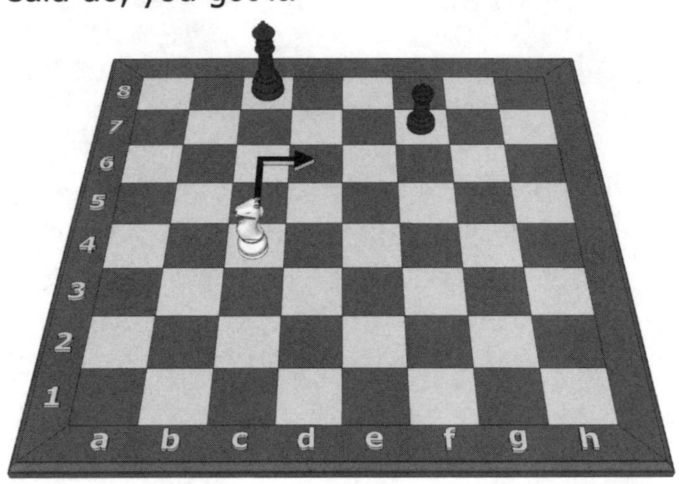

A "family fork" is when you attack more than two pieces at once. Look at the position of the pieces on the board here. A family fork is possible. Do you see it? Okay then ...

What is the best square to put the Black **N**?

Did you find f3? If you did, that's great.

The Skewer

Here, the White **B** can make a move called a "skewer." A skewer is when one piece is attacked but, if it is moved to safety, the skewer-ing piece attacks a second piece that was behind it!

What is the best square for the **B**?

You got it again - g2!

The move "skewers" both pawns. Imagine a stick through them. Doesn't it look like a "shish-kabob?" Let's look at another.

Skewer these two rooks with the White **B**. Move it to f2. Even if you don't threaten a check, you will win a **R**.

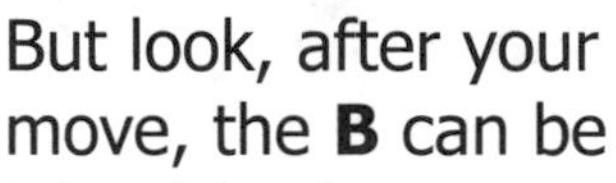

But look, after your move, the **B** can be taken! Losing your capturing piece on the very next move is called an "exchange."

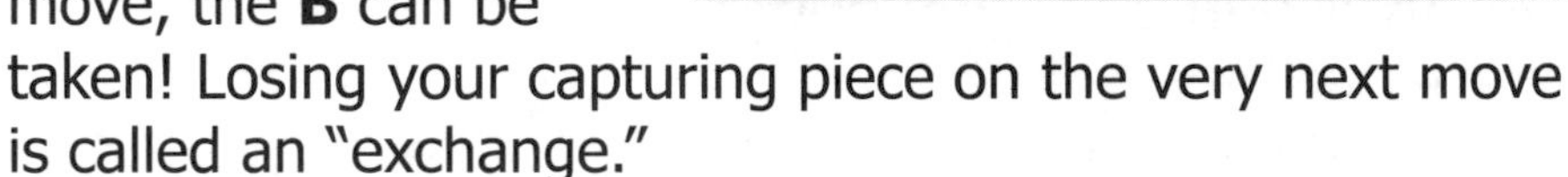

So should you have taken the **R** if you risked losing the **B** in the very next move? Think about it. Even if you lost the **B**, you'd have won a **R** for it.

Capturing a **R** for a **N** or a **B** is called "winning the exchange." You will win a **R**, and the most Black can get here is a **B**. **R**s are worth more then **B**s, so that is a good move for White.

You can review the value of the pieces below.

Remember that your **K** is priceless!

PIECE	SYMBOL	VALUE IN PAWNS
Q	♛	9
R	♜	5
B	♝	3
N	♞	3
p	♟	1

Discovery

Here is a strong attacking position called a "discovery." Look closely at the board and see if you can find — or discover — it.

When the **B** makes a move to anywhere on the board, the **R** will be checking the White **K**. This is a "discovered check."

Double Check

If getting a check is fun, getting a double check is double the fun, right? Here the **N** to c5 move is a double check. Both the **N** and the **R** are checking the **K**.

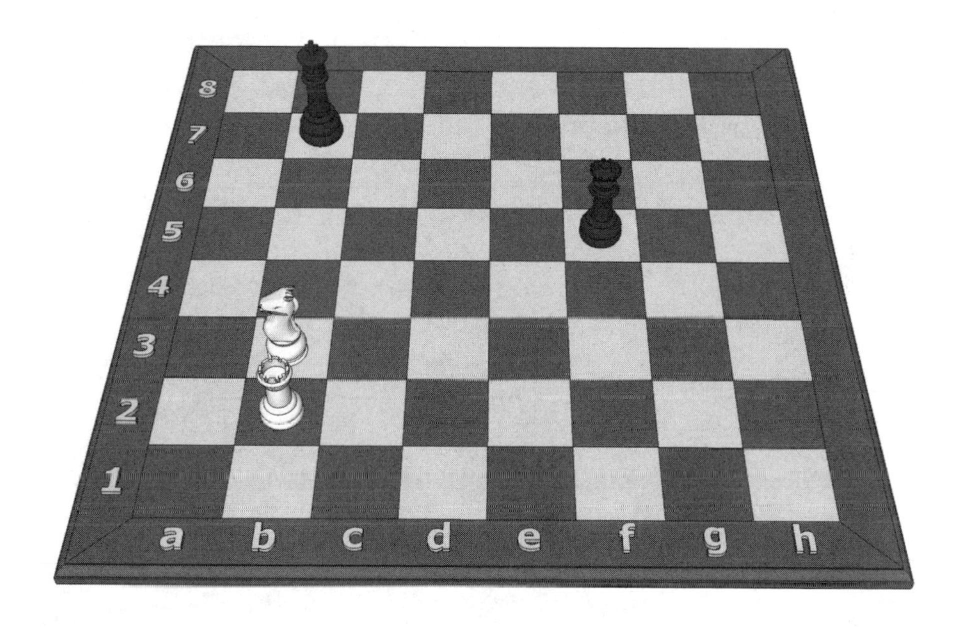

But look again! Even better is the **N** to d4 move. The **R** is still checking the **K**, but the **N** will capture the **Q** on the next move!

How's that for cool?

Double Stuff

In life, sometimes it's better to do one thing at a time. Other times you can do two things at once — like sing a song while you're drying dishes.

In chess, it's good to have more than one thing happening on the board at a time. Let's look at some ways you can do this "double stuff."

Here, the White **Q** is threatening to take Black's pawn on b7.

Black moves the **B** to c6, protecting the pawn

and

threatening mate with **Q** captures g2 (this is written as Qxg2 or Qg2).

If the White pawn on f2 moves to f3, the **B** can just take it. The g-pawn is pinned by the Black **Q**, so it can't re-capture.

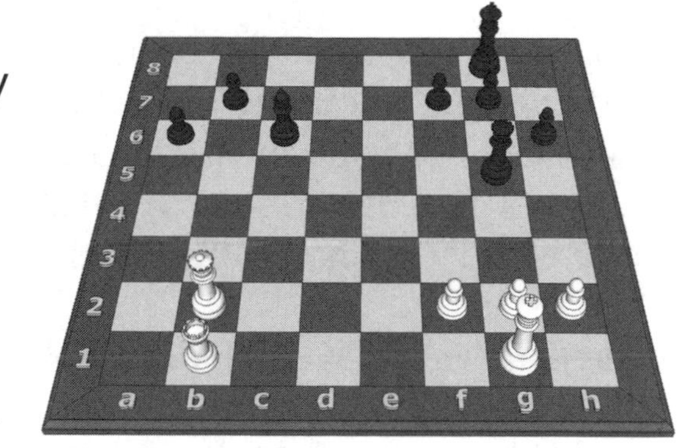

The **B** move (Bc6) by Black causes White big trouble.

When you look at the board, see if you can do two things at once with a move. If you are threatening to take a piece at the same time as you are threatening mate, you will almost definitely win the game.

Here, if you are White, move Qc2, threatening Qxc8 and Qxh7 mate!

Your opponent now has a choice to make — either save the **K**, or save the piece.

III. A FUN GAME

Now, we'll go over a game one move at a time. The shaded moves show the move in the diagram next to it. You can use your chessboard when you go over the moves, or just use your book. Make sure to look at every move and decide how you would move.

This game was played in 1989 at the U.S. Amateur Team Championship in New Jersey. This tournament is played every February on President's Weekend. The tournament got so big (more than 1000 players), CA, FL and MI started having the same event at the same time, every year. Lots of kids play in this event. White was played by David Koenig. Black was played by Charles Pole.

Chess Notation Code

K King	! good move
Q Queen	!! great move
R Rook	? bad move
B Bishop	?? rotten move
N Knight	?! may be a bad move
X captures or takes	!? interesting move
+ check	0-0 castle kingside
++ checkmate	0-0-0 castle queenside

	White	Black
1	e4	e5
2	Nf3	Nc6
3	Bb5	a6
4	Ba4	d6
5	c3	f5
6	ef5	Bf5
7	d4	e4
8	Ng5	Be7
9	Qb3	Bg5
10	Bg5	Qg5
11	Qb7	Qc1+
12	Ke2	Qh1
13	Qa8+	Kf7
14	Bc6	Ne7
15	Qh8	Nc6
16	Qa8	Bg4+
17	f3	ef3+
18	gf3	Qf3+
	resigns	

1. e4

1...e5

This game uses a popular opening called the "Ruy Lopez."

	White	Black
1	e4	e5
2	Nf3	Nc6
3	Bb5	a6
4	Ba4	d6
5	c3	f5
6	ef5	Bf5
7	d4	e4
8	Ng5	Be7
9	Qb3	Bg5
10	Bg5	Qg5
11	Qb7	Qc1+
12	Ke2	Qh1
13	Qa8+	Kf7
14	Bc6	Ne7
15	Qh8	Nc6
16	Qa8	Bg4+
17	f3	ef3+
18	gf3	Qf3+
	resigns	

2.Nf3

2...Nc6

	White	Black
1	e4	e5
2	Nf3	Nc6
3	Bb5	a6
4	Ba4	d6
5	c3	f5
6	ef5	Bf5
7	d4	e4
8	Ng5	Be7
9	Qb3	Bg5
10	Bg5	Qg5
11	Qb7	Qc1+
12	Ke2	Qh1
13	Qa8+	Kf7
14	Bc6	Ne7
15	Qh8	Nc6
16	Qa8	Bg4+
17	f3	ef3+
18	gf3	Qf3+
	resigns	

3.Bb5

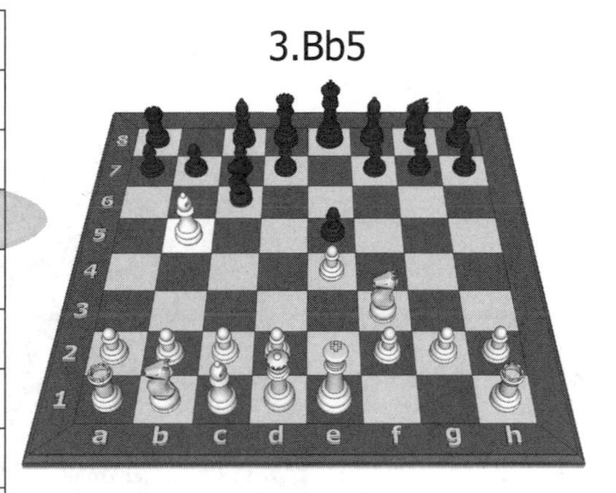

3...a6

	White	Black
1	e4	e5
2	Nf3	Nc6
3	Bb5	a6
4	Ba4	d6
5	c3	f5
6	ef5	Bf5
7	d4	e4
8	Ng5	Be7
9	Qb3	Bg5
10	Bg5	Qg5
11	Qb7	Qc1+
12	Ke2	Qh1
13	Qa8+	Kf7
14	Bc6	Ne7
15	Qh8	Nc6
16	Qa8	Bg4+
17	f3	ef3+
18	gf3	Qf3+
	resigns	

4.Ba4

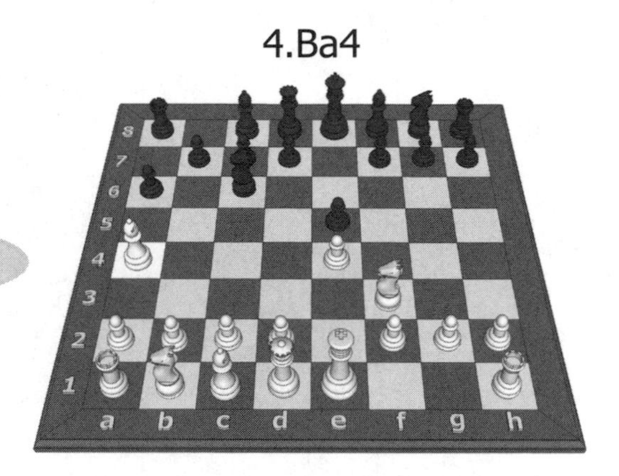

4...d6

	White	Black
1	e4	e5
2	Nf3	Nc6
3	Bb5	a6
4	Ba4	d6
5	c3	f5
6	ef5	Bf5
7	d4	e4
8	Ng5	Be7
9	Qb3	Bg5
10	Bg5	Qg5
11	Qb7	Qc1+
12	Ke2	Qh1
13	Qa8+	Kf7
14	Bc6	Ne7
15	Qh8	Nc6
16	Qa8	Bg4+
17	f3	ef3+
18	gf3	Qf3+
	resigns	

5.c3

5...f5

These first five moves are very ordinary. Lots of books show games with this position. Black is trying for an open position on this move.

	White	Black
1	e4	e5
2	Nf3	Nc6
3	Bb5	a6
4	Ba4	d6
5	c3	f5
6	ef5	Bf5
7	d4	e4
8	Ng5	Be7
9	Qb3	Bg5
10	Bg5	Qg5
11	Qb7	Qc1+
12	Ke2	Qh1
13	Qa8+	Kf7
14	Bc6	Ne7
15	Qh8	Nc6
16	Qa8	Bg4+
17	f3	ef3+
18	gf3	Qf3+
	resigns	

6.ef5

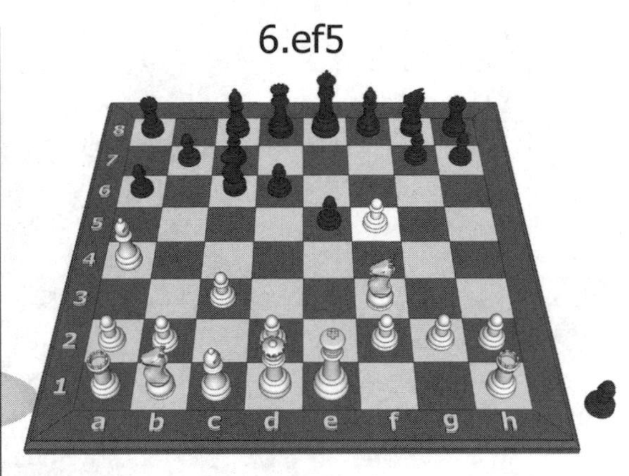

6...Bf5

	White	Black
1	e4	e5
2	Nf3	Nc6
3	Bb5	a6
4	Ba4	d6
5	c3	f5
6	ef5	Bf5
7	d4	e4
8	Ng5	Be7
9	Qb3	Bg5
10	Bg5	Qg5
11	Qb7	Qc1+
12	Ke2	Qh1
13	Qa8+	Kf7
14	Bc6	Ne7
15	Qh8	Nc6
16	Qa8	Bg4+
17	f3	ef3+
18	gf3	Qf3+
	resigns	

7.d4

White is trying to open the position.

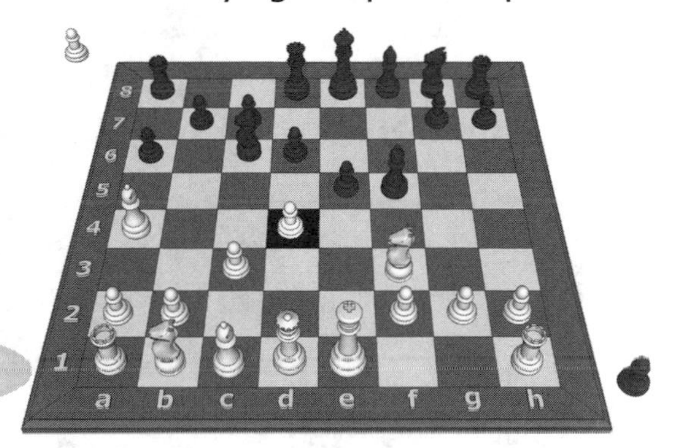

7...e4

Instead of taking White's pawn, Black attacks the **N**.

	White	Black
1	e4	e5
2	Nf3	Nc6
3	Bb5	a6
4	Ba4	d6
5	c3	f5
6	ef5	Bf5
7	d4	e4
8	Ng5	Be7
9	Qb3	Bg5
10	Bg5	Qg5
11	Qb7	Qc1+
12	Ke2	Qh1
13	Qa8+	Kf7
14	Bc6	Ne7
15	Qh8	Nc6
16	Qa8	Bg4+
17	f3	ef3+
18	gf3	Qf3+
	resigns	

8.Ng5

8...Be7

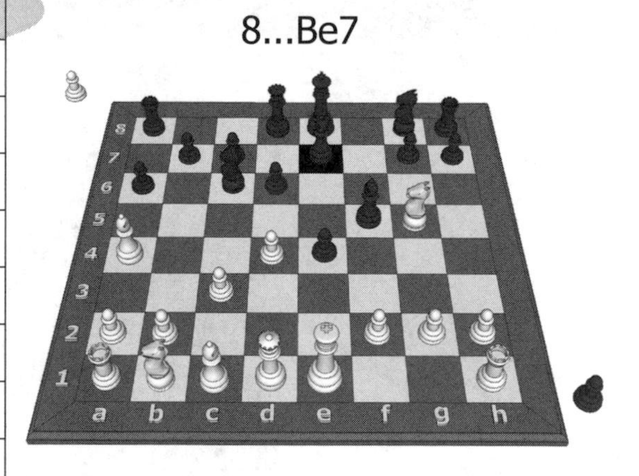

Black attacks the **N** with the **Q** and the **B**.

Instead of protecting the **N**, White attacks. It's a double threat! The **Q** threatens to check at f7 and to capture the pawn on b7.

	White	Black
1	e4	e5
2	Nf3	Nc6
3	Bb5	a6
4	Ba4	d6
5	c3	f5
6	ef5	Bf5
7	d4	e4
8	Ng5	Be7
9	Qb3	Bg5
10	Bg5	Qg5
11	Qb7	Qc1+
12	Ke2	Qh1
13	Qa8+	Kf7
14	Bc6	Ne7
15	Qh8	Nc6
16	Qa8	Bg4+
17	f3	ef3+
18	gf3	Qf3+
	resigns	

9.Qb3

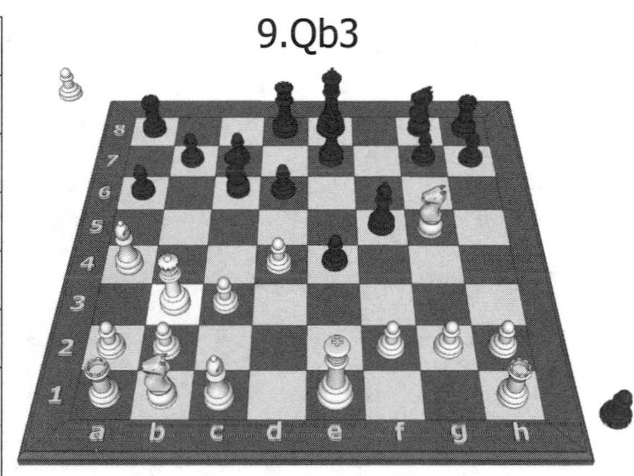

9...Bg5

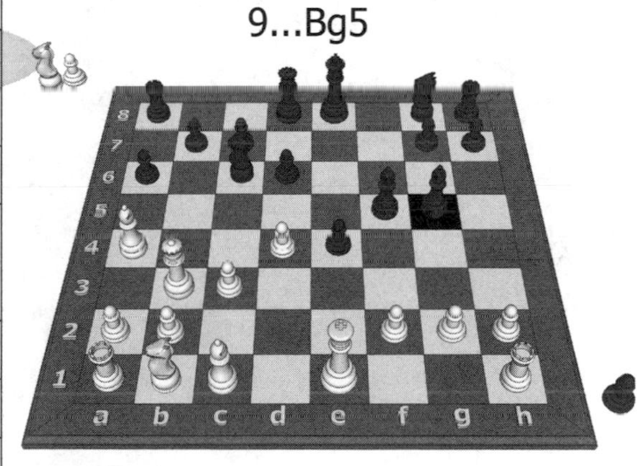

Black ignores both threats, captures the White **N**, and attacks the **B** on c1.

	White	Black
1	e4	e5
2	Nf3	Nc6
3	Bb5	a6
4	Ba4	d6
5	c3	f5
6	ef5	Bf5
7	d4	e4
8	Ng5	Be7
9	Qb3	Bg5
10	Bg5	Qg5
11	Qb7	Qc1+
12	Ke2	Qh1
13	Qa8+	Kf7
14	Bc6	Ne7
15	Qh8	Nc6
16	Qa8	Bg4+
17	f3	ef3+
18	gf3	Qf3+
	resigns	

10.Bg5

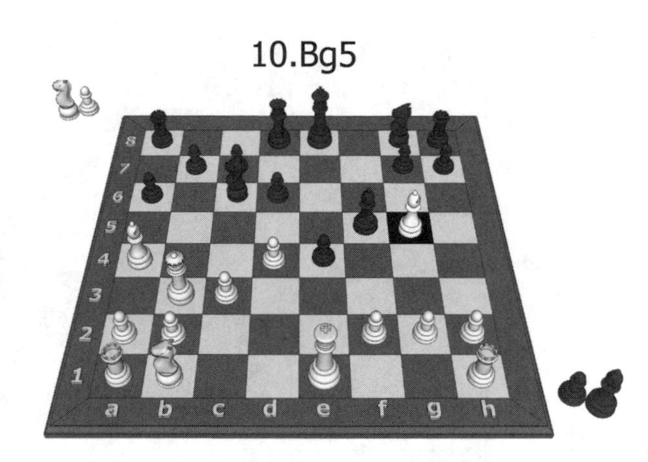

10...Qg5

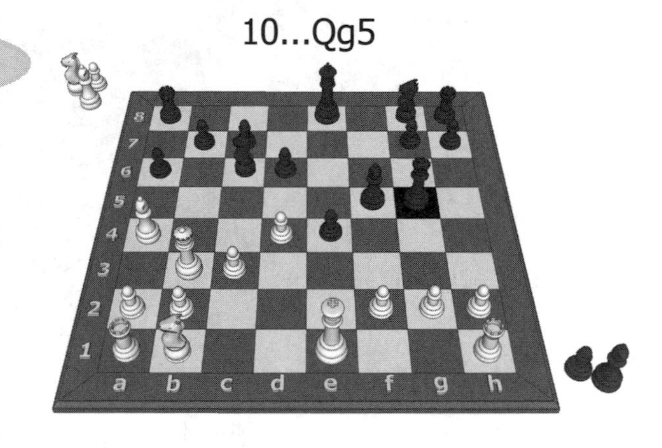

The **Q** takes the pawn and threatens the **R** on a8 and the **N** on c6.

	White	Black
1	e4	e5
2	Nf3	Nc6
3	Bb5	a6
4	Ba4	d6
5	c3	f5
6	ef5	Bf5
7	d4	e4
8	Ng5	Be7
9	Qb3	Bg5
10	Bg5	Qg5
11	Qb7	Qc1+
12	Kc2	Qh1
13	Qa8+	Kf7
14	Bc6	Ne7
15	Qh8	Nc6
16	Qa8	Bg4+
17	f3	ef3+
18	gf3	Qf3+
	resigns	

11.Qb7

11...Qc1+

Instead of trying to protect the pieces, Black attacks the White **K**. Check!

This move, the only one for White's **K**, leaves White's **R** hanging.

	White	Black
1	e4	e5
2	Nf3	Nc6
3	Bb5	a6
4	Ba4	d6
5	c3	f5
6	ef5	Bf5
7	d4	e4
8	Ng5	Be7
9	Qb3	Bg5
10	Bg5	Qg5
11	Qb7	Qc1+
12	Ke2	Qh1
13	Qa8+	Kf7
14	Bc6	Ne7
15	Qh8	Nc6
16	Qa8	Bg4+
17	f3	ef3+
18	gf3	Qf3+
	resigns	

12.Ke2

12...Qh1

The Black **Q** captures the White **R** on h1. Now the Black **R** on a8 and the Black **N** on c6 are both hanging. They are completely unprotected.

Plenty of stuff to look at in this game isn't there?

White must feel good about getting Black's **R** and checking at the same time.

	White	Black
1	e4	e5
2	Nf3	Nc6
3	Bb5	a6
4	Ba4	d6
5	c3	f5
6	ef5	Bf5
7	d4	e4
8	Ng5	Be7
9	Qb3	Bg5
10	Bg5	Qg5
11	Qb7	Qc1+
12	Ke2	Qh1
13	Qa8+	Kf7
14	Bc6	Ne7
15	Qh8	Nc6
16	Qa8	Bg4+
17	f3	ef3+
18	gf3	Qf3+
	resigns	

13.Qa8+

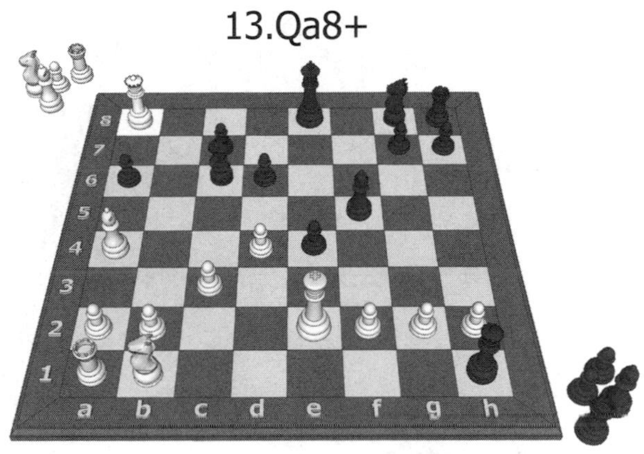

13...Kf7

Oops! White captured Black's **N**.

	White	Black
1	e4	e5
2	Nf3	Nc6
3	Bb5	a6
4	Ba4	d6
5	c3	f5
6	ef5	Bf5
7	d4	e4
8	Ng5	Be7
9	Qb3	Bg5
10	Bg5	Qg5
11	Qb7	Qc1+
12	Ke2	Qh1
13	Qa8+	Kf7
14	Bc6	Ne7
15	Qh8	Nc6
16	Qa8	Bg4+
17	f3	ef3+
18	gf3	Qf3+
	resigns	

14.Bc6

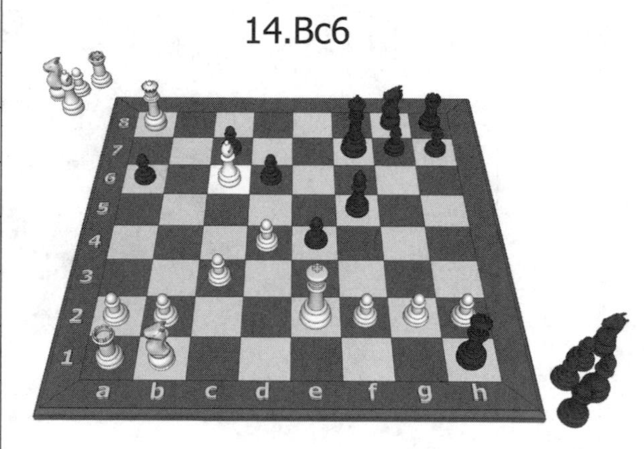

14...Ne7

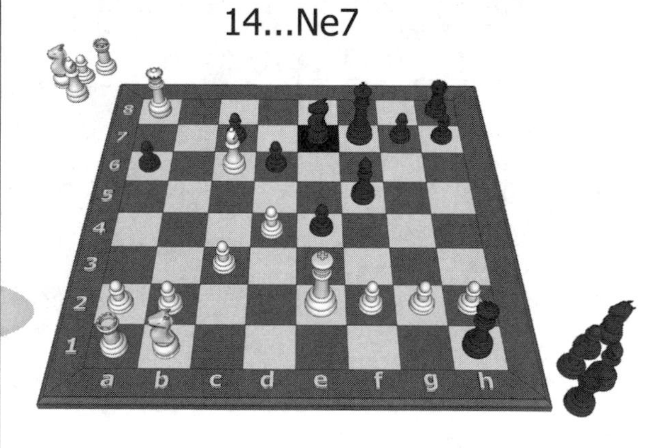

Black lets White capture the **R**, but gets another piece into the fight.

And another **R** bites the dust.

	White	Black
1	e4	e5
2	Nf3	Nc6
3	Bb5	a6
4	Ba4	d6
5	c3	f5
6	ef5	Bf5
7	d4	e4
8	Ng5	Be7
9	Qb3	Bg5
10	Bg5	Qg5
11	Qb7	Qc1+
12	Ke2	Qh1
13	Qa8+	Kf7
14	Bc6	Ne7
15	Qh8	Nc6
16	Qa8	Bg4+
17	f3	ef3+
18	gf3	Qf3+
	resigns	

15.Qh8

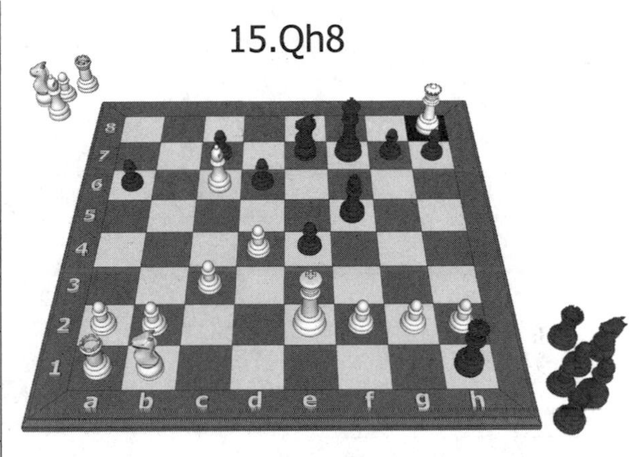

15...Nc6

White attacks the **N**.

	White	Black
1	e4	e5
2	Nf3	Nc6
3	Bb5	a6
4	Ba4	d6
5	c3	f5
6	ef5	Bf5
7	d4	e4
8	Ng5	Be7
9	Qb3	Bg5
10	Bg5	Qg5
11	Qb7	Qc1+
12	Ke2	Qh1
13	Qa8+	Kf7
14	Bc6	Ne7
15	Qh8	Nc6
16	Qa8	Bg4+
17	f3	ef3+
18	gf3	Qf3+
	resigns	

16.Qa8

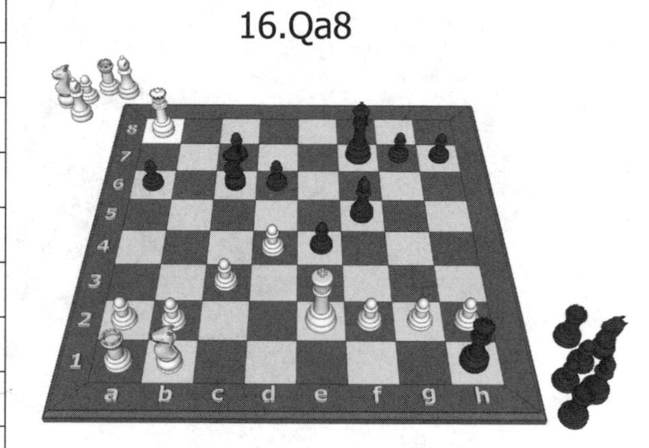

16...Bg4+

Black checks with the **B**.

White is in big trouble. The check is blocked with the White pawn.

	White	Black
1	e4	e5
2	Nf3	Nc6
3	Bb5	a6
4	Ba4	d6
5	c3	f5
6	ef5	Bf5
7	d4	e4
8	Ng5	Be7
9	Qb3	Bg5
10	Bg5	Qg5
11	Qb7	Qc1+
12	Ke2	Qh1
13	Qa8+	Kf7
14	Bc6	Ne7
15	Qh8	Nc6
16	Qa8	Bg4+
17	f3	ef3+
18	gf3	Qf3+
	resigns	

17. f3

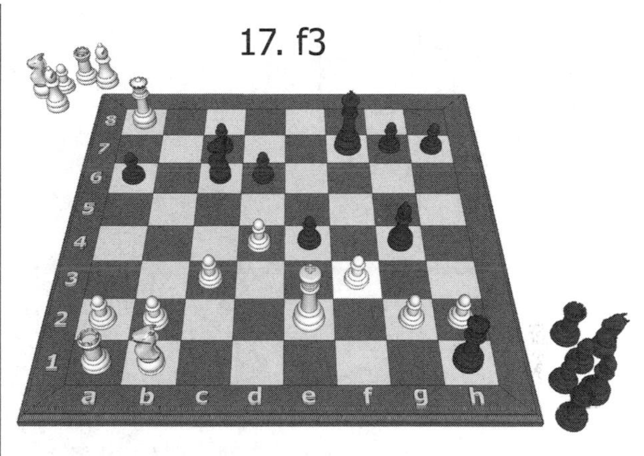

17...ef3+

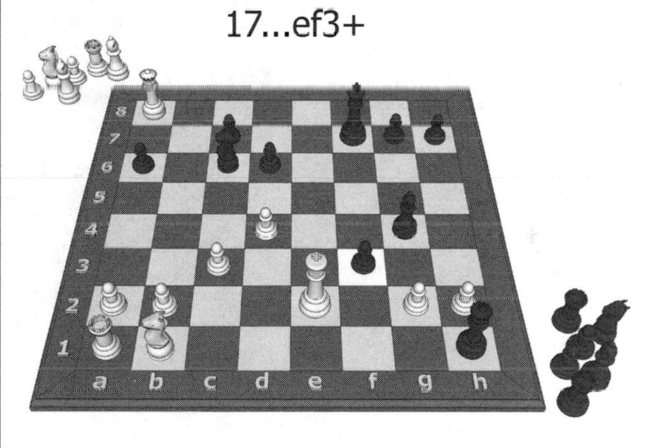

Black captures the pawn with a check.

White recaptures and again blocks the check. Black now has two pieces attacking the pawn.

	White	Black
1	e4	e5
2	Nf3	Nc6
3	Bb5	a6
4	Ba4	d6
5	c3	f5
6	ef5	Bf5
7	d4	e4
8	Ng5	Be7
9	Qb3	Bg5
10	Bg5	Qg5
11	Qb7	Qc1+
12	Ke2	Qh1
13	Qa8+	Kf7
14	Bc6	Ne7
15	Qh8	Nc6
16	Qa8	Bg4+
17	f3	ef3+
18	gf3	Qf3+
	resigns	

18.gf3

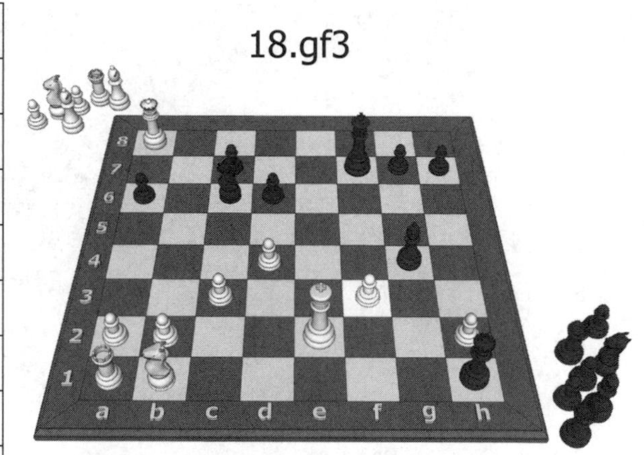

18...Qf3+

Black's **Q** is protected by the **B**.

White sees no way to stop checkmate. At what would have been move 19, White resigns.

Look again, here, at the last board.

If play had gone on, after the White **K** moves to d2, the Black **Q** would check at e2. The White **K** must then go to c1, and the **Q** would checkmate on d1. End of story.

IV. A WEIRD GAME

Here, we'll go over another game; you'll see that it's really different from the game we just went through. Go over it in the same way you did the last one — one move at a time.

This game was played in 1975. Pete Tamburro played White and Vincent Klemm played Black. Both players grew to be very important in the chess world. Pete is an award-winning chess journalist, writer and teacher. Vincent is a Master chess player, teacher, and an authority on chess books, computer chess and equipment.

	White	Black
1	e4	c5
2	c3	g6
3	d4	cd4
4	cd4	d5
5	e5	Nc6
6	Nc3	Nh6
7	h4	Nf5
8	Be3	h5
9	Rc1	Bg7
10	Nf3	0-0
11	Bb5	Bd7!
12	Nd5	Qa5+
13	Nc3	Ne5!!
14	de5	Bb5
15	Qd5	a6
16	a4	Rfd8
17	Qc5	Rac8
18	Qb6	Ne3!
19	Qe3	Rd3
20	Qe4	Rdc3
21	bc3	Rc3
22	Rc3	Qc3+
23	Nd2	Qc1
		mate

This opening is called the Sicilian Defense. Openings using the word "defense" means the black moves set the tone for the whole game.

1.e4

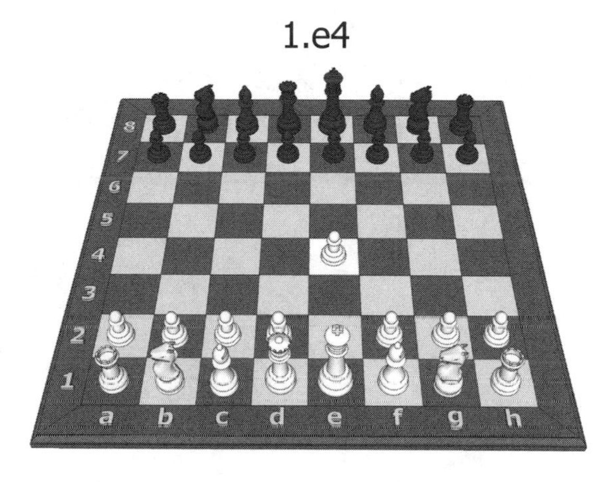

1...c5

	White	Black
1	e4	c5
2	c3	g6
3	d4	cd4
4	cd4	d5
5	e5	Nc6
6	Nc3	Nh6
7	h4	Nf5
8	Be3	h5
9	Rc1	Bg7
10	Nf3	0-0
11	Bb5	Bd7!
12	Nd5	Qa5+
13	Nc3	Ne5!!
14	de5	Bb5
15	Qd5	a6
16	a4	Rfd8
17	Qc5	Rac8
18	Qb6	Ne3!
19	Qe3	Rd3
20	Qe4	Rdc3
21	bc3	Rc3
22	Rc3	Qc3+
23	Nd2	Qc1
		mate

2.c3

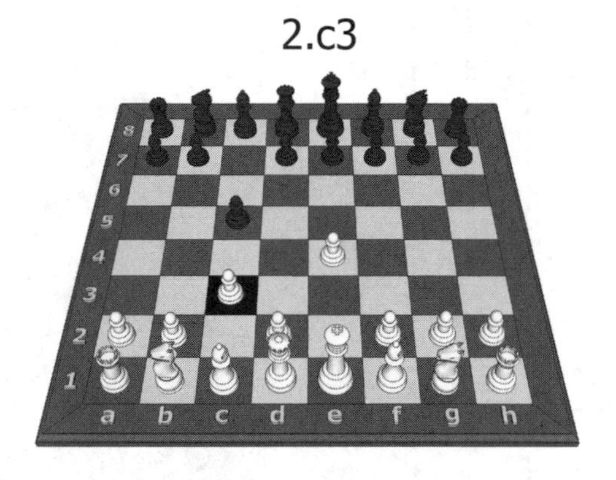

2...g6

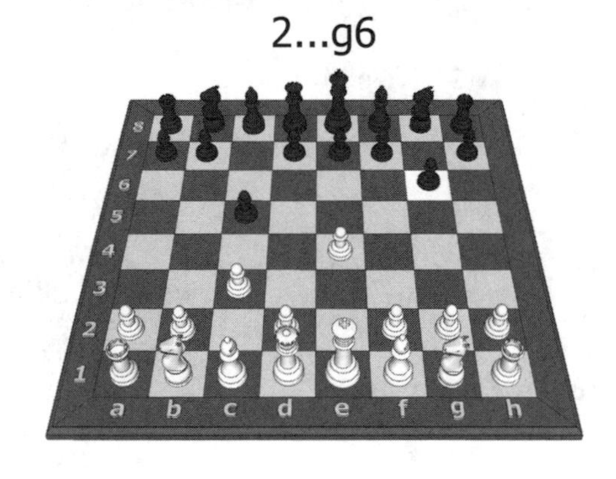

	White	Black
1	e4	c5
2	c3	g6
3	d4	cd4
4	cd4	d5
5	e5	Nc6
6	Nc3	Nh6
7	h4	Nf5
8	Be3	h5
9	Rc1	Bg7
10	Nf3	0-0
11	Bb5	Bd7!
12	Nd5	Qa5+
13	Nc3	Ne5!!
14	de5	Bb5
15	Qd5	a6
16	a4	Rfd8
17	Qc5	Rac8
18	Qb6	Ne3!
19	Qe3	Rd3
20	Qe4	Rdc3
21	bc3	Rc3
22	Rc3	Qc3+
23	Nd2	Qc1
		mate

Look at all the squares where White's **B**'s can go. It's great for White if this is an open game.

3.d4

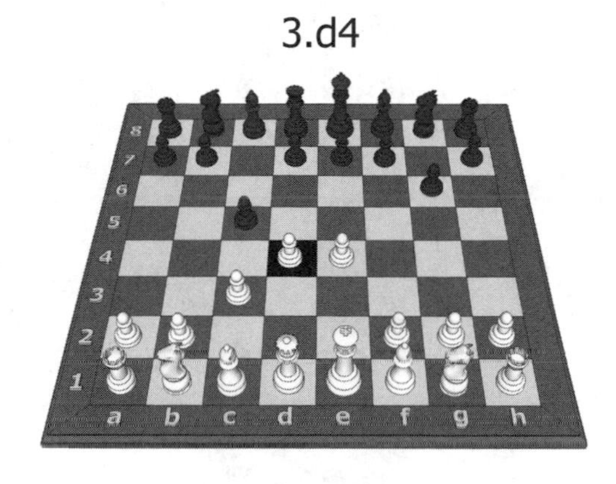

3...cd4

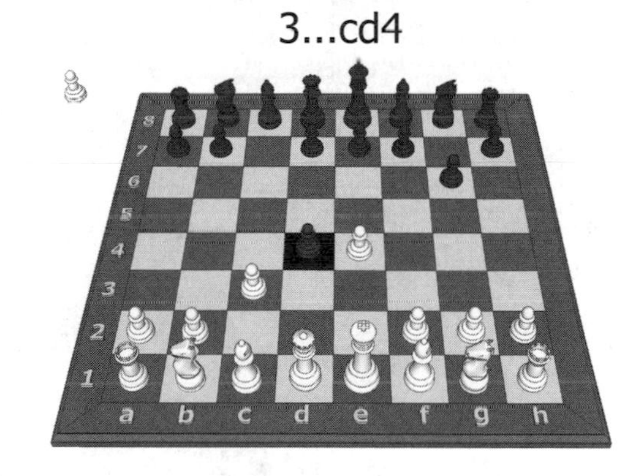

	White	Black
1	e4	c5
2	c3	g6
3	d4	cd4
4	cd4	d5
5	e5	Nc6
6	Nc3	Nh6
7	h4	Nf5
8	Be3	h5
9	Rc1	Bg7
10	Nf3	0-0
11	Bb5	Bd7!
12	Nd5	Qa5+
13	Nc3	Ne5!!
14	de5	Bb5
15	Qd5	a6
16	a4	Rfd8
17	Qc5	Rac8
18	Qb6	Ne3!
19	Qe3	Rd3
20	Qe4	Rdc3
21	bc3	Rc3
22	Rc3	Qc3+
23	Nd2	Qc1
		mate

4.cd4

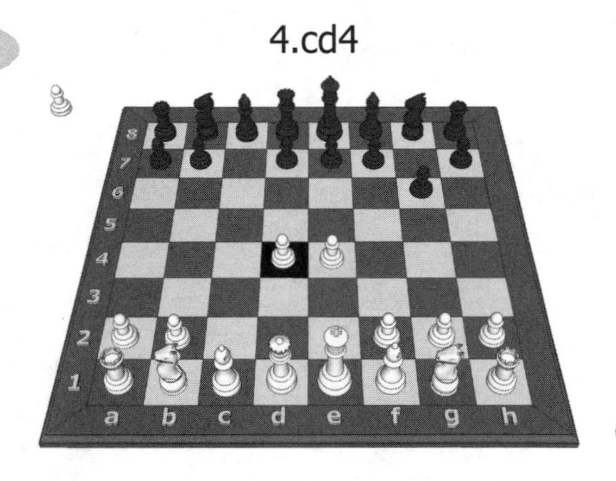

4...d5

	White	Black
1	e4	c5
2	c3	g6
3	d4	cd4
4	cd4	d5
5	e5	Nc6
6	Nc3	Nh6
7	h4	Nf5
8	Be3	h5
9	Rc1	Bg7
10	Nf3	0-0
11	Bb5	Bd7!
12	Nd5	Qa5+
13	Nc3	Ne5!!
14	de5	Bb5
15	Qd5	a6
16	a4	Rfd8
17	Qc5	Rac8
18	Qb6	Ne3!
19	Qe3	Rd3
20	Qe4	Rdc3
21	bc3	Rc3
22	Rc3	Qc3+
23	Nd2	Qc1
		mate

White closes the position up a little.

5.e5

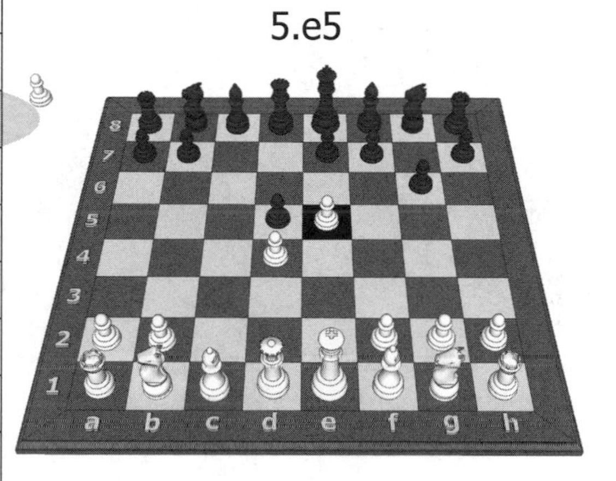

5...Nc6

Black might have some trouble moving around.

	White	Black
1	e4	c5
2	c3	g6
3	d4	cd4
4	cd4	d5
5	e5	Nc6
6	Nc3	Nh6
7	h4	Nf5
8	Be3	h5
9	Rc1	Bg7
10	Nf3	0-0
11	Bb5	Bd7!
12	Nd5	Qa5+
13	Nc3	Ne5!!
14	de5	Bb5
15	Qd5	a6
16	a4	Rfd8
17	Qc5	Rac8
18	Qb6	Ne3!
19	Qe3	Rd3
20	Qe4	Rdc3
21	bc3	Rc3
22	Rc3	Qc3+
23	Nd2	Qc1
		mate

6.Nc3

6...Nh6

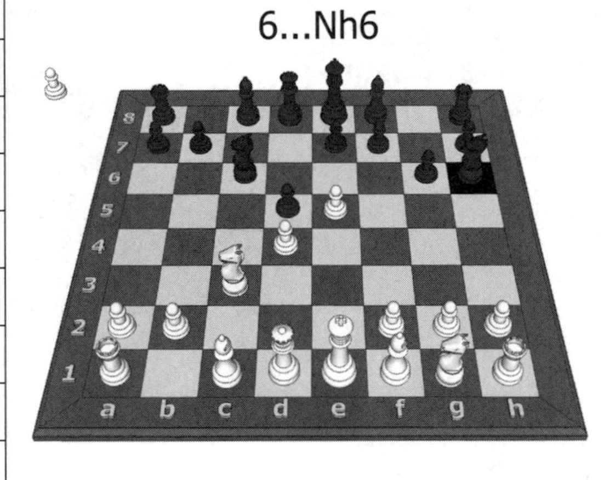

The Black **N** is on a bad square at h6, but the plan is to move it to f5 as soon as possible.

	White	Black
1	e4	c5
2	c3	g6
3	d4	cd4
4	cd4	d5
5	e5	Nc6
6	Nc3	Nh6
7	h4	Nf5
8	Be3	h5
9	Rc1	Bg7
10	Nf3	0-0
11	Bb5	Bd7!
12	Nd5	Qa5+
13	Nc3	Ne5!!
14	de5	Bb5
15	Qd5	a6
16	a4	Rfd8
17	Qc5	Rac8
18	Qb6	Ne3!
19	Qe3	Rd3
20	Qe4	Rdc3
21	bc3	Rc3
22	Rc3	Qc3+
23	Nd2	Qc1
		mate

7.h4

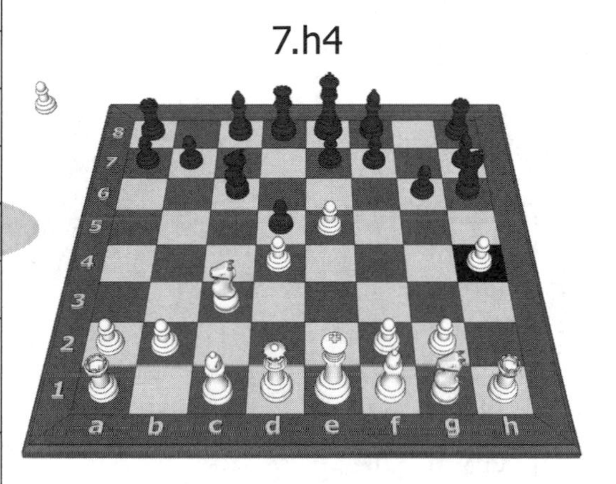

7...Nf5

Now Black is attacking the pawn on d4 with two pieces.

	White	Black
1	e4	c5
2	c3	g6
3	d4	cd4
4	cd4	d5
5	e5	Nc6
6	Nc3	Nh6
7	h4	Nf5
8	Be3	h5
9	Rc1	Bg7
10	Nf3	0-0
11	Bb5	Bd7!
12	Nd5	Qa5+
13	Nc3	Ne5!!
14	de5	Bb5
15	Qd5	a6
16	a4	Rfd8
17	Qc5	Rac8
18	Qb6	Ne3!
19	Qe3	Rd3
20	Qe4	Rdc3
21	bc3	Rc3
22	Rc3	Qc3+
23	Nd2	Qc1
		mate

White protects the pawn.

8.Be3

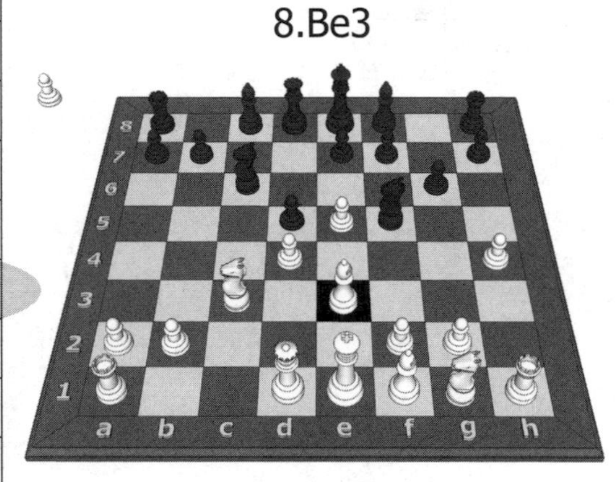

8...h5

Black keeps the white **g**-pawn from attacking the **N**, and keeps the **h**-pawn from moving forward.

	White	Black
1	e4	c5
2	c3	g6
3	d4	cd4
4	cd4	d5
5	e5	Nc6
6	Nc3	Nh6
7	h4	Nf5
8	Be3	h5
9	Rc1	Bg7
10	Nf3	0-0
11	Bb5	Bd7!
12	Nd5	Qd5+
13	Nc3	Ne5!!
14	de5	Bb5
15	Qd5	a6
16	a4	Rfd8
17	Qc5	Rac8
18	Qb6	Ne3!
19	Qe3	Rd3
20	Qe4	Rdc3
21	bc3	Rc3
22	Rc3	Qc3+
23	Nd2	Qc1
		mate

9.Rc1

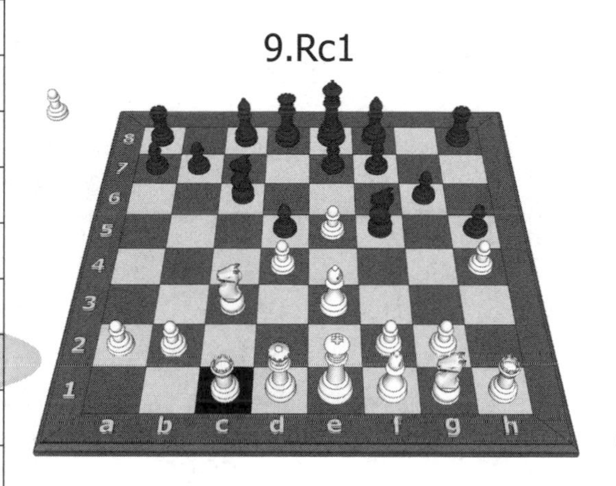

9...Bg7

	White	Black
1	e4	c5
2	c3	g6
3	d4	cd4
4	cd4	d5
5	e5	Nc6
6	Nc3	Nh6
7	h4	Nf5
8	Be3	h5
9	Rc1	Bg7
10	Nf3	0-0
11	Bb5	Bd7!
12	Nd5	Qa5+
13	Nc3	Ne5!!
14	de5	Bb5
15	Qd5	a6
16	a4	Rfd8
17	Qc5	Rac8
18	Qb6	Ne3!
19	Qe3	Rd3
20	Qe4	Rdc3
21	bc3	Rc3
22	Rc3	Qc3+
23	Nd2	Qc1
		mate

10.Nf3

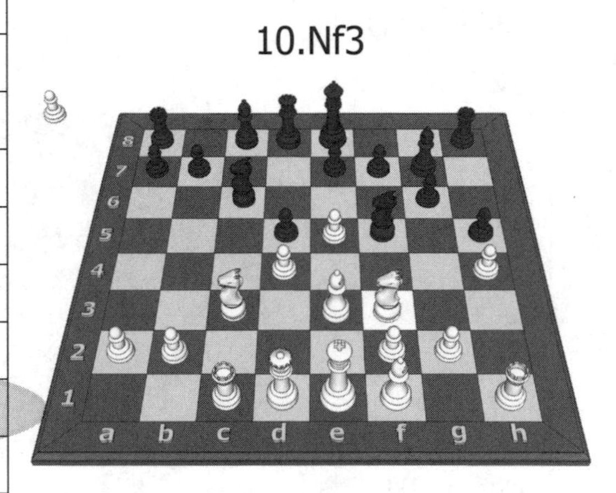

10...0-0

A kingside castle. Black is setting a trap here. Watch carefully.

	White	Black
1	e4	c5
2	c3	g6
3	d4	cd4
4	cd4	d5
5	e5	Nc6
6	Nc3	Nh6
7	h4	Nf5
8	Be3	h5
9	Rc1	Bg7
10	Nf3	0-0
11	Bb5	Bd7!
12	Nd5	Qa5+
13	Nc3	Ne5!!
14	de5	Bb5
15	Qd5	a6
16	a4	Rfd8
17	Qc5	Rac8
18	Qb6	Ne3!
19	Qe3	Rd3
20	Qe4	Rdc3
21	bc3	Rc3
22	Rc3	Qc3+
23	Nd2	Qc1
		mate

11.Bb5

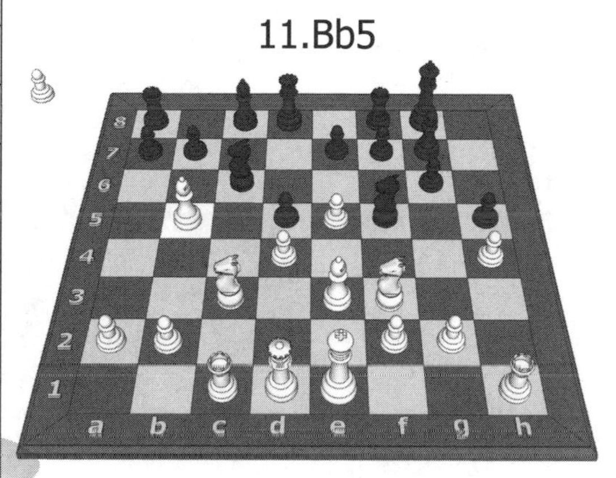

11...Bd7!

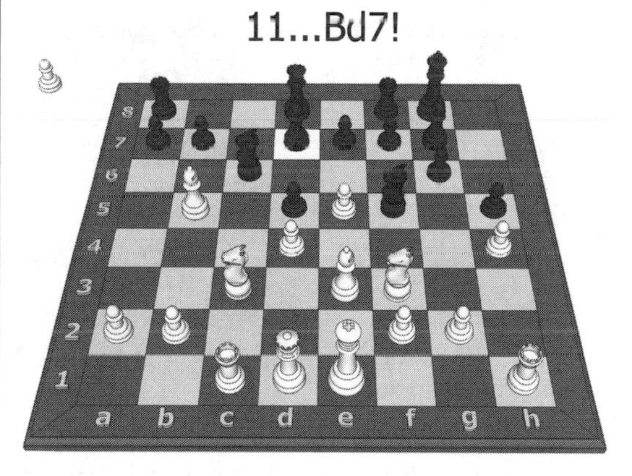

	White	Black
1	e4	c5
2	c3	g6
3	d4	cd4
4	cd4	d5
5	e5	Nc6
6	Nc3	Nh6
7	h4	Nf5
8	Be3	h5
9	Rc1	Bg7
10	Nf3	0-0
11	Bb5	Bd7!
12	Nd5	Qa5+
13	Nc3	Ne5!!
14	de5	Bb5
15	Qd5	a6
16	a4	Rfd8
17	Qc5	Rac8
18	Qb6	Ne3!
19	Qe3	Rd3
20	Qe4	Rdc3
21	bc3	Rc3+
22	Rc3	Qc3
23	Nd2	Qc1
		mate

12.Nd5

12...Qa5+

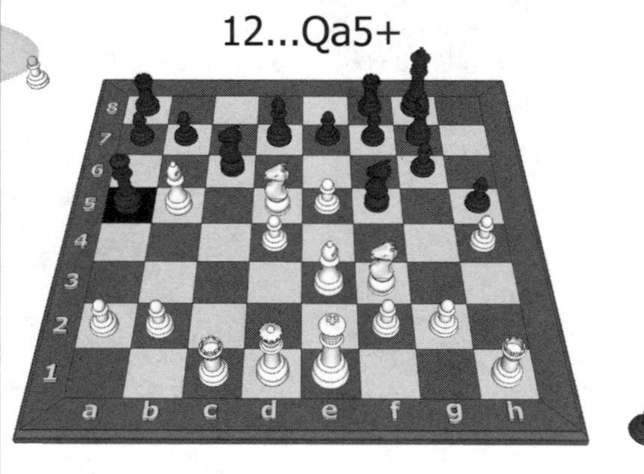

White is being really greedy, but Black shows it won't work here. This is known as "refuting" a move. You're telling the opponent "ha — that didn't work."

	White	Black
1	e4	c5
2	c3	g6
3	d4	cd4
4	cd4	d5
5	e5	Nc6
6	Nc3	Nh6
7	h4	Nf5
8	Be3	h5
9	Rc1	Bg7
10	Nf3	0-0
11	Bb5	Bd7!
12	Nd5	Qa5+
13	Nc3	Ne5!!
14	de5	Bb5
15	Qd5	a6
16	a4	Rfd8
17	Qc5	Rac8
18	Qb6	Ne3!
19	Qe3	Rd3
20	Qe4	Rdc3
21	bc3	Rc3
22	Rc3	Qc3+
23	Nd2	Qc1
		mate

13.Nc3

13...Ne5!!

It looks as if Black is sacrificing the **N**, giving it away. But the White **B** on b5 is being attacked by two pieces.

	White	Black
1	e4	c5
2	c3	g6
3	d4	cd4
4	cd4	d5
5	e5	Nc6
6	Nc3	Nh6
7	h4	Nf5
8	Be3	h5
9	Rc1	Bg7
10	Nf3	0-0
11	Bb5	Bd7!
12	Nd5	Qa5+
13	Nc3	Ne5!!
14	de5	Bb5
15	Qd5	a6
16	a4	Rfd8
17	Qc5	Rac8
18	Qb6	Ne3!
19	Qe3	Rd3
20	Qe4	Rdc3
21	bc3	Rc3
22	Rc3	Qc3+
23	Nd2	Qc1
		mate

White wins the **N**.

14.de5

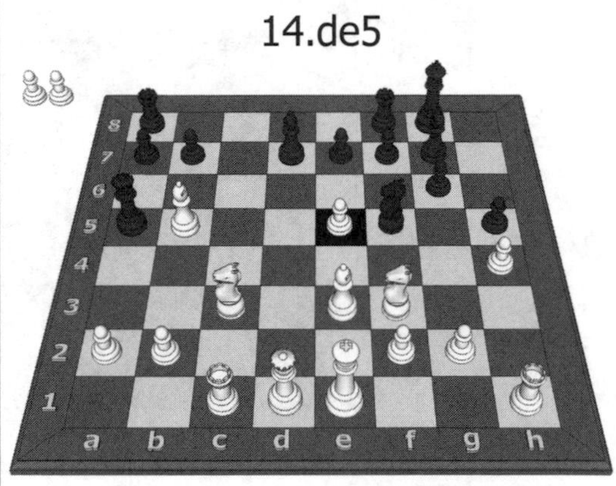

14...Bb5

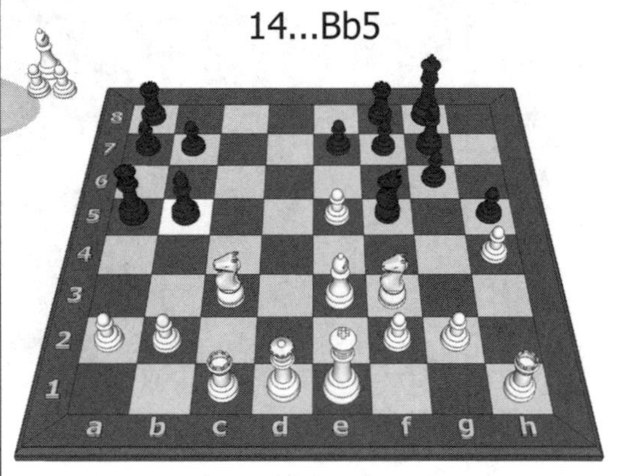

But White also loses the **B**.

	White	Black
1	e4	c5
2	c3	g6
3	d4	cd4
4	cd4	d5
5	e5	Nc6
6	Nc3	Nh6
7	h4	Nf5
8	Be3	h5
9	Rc1	Bg7
10	Nf3	0-0
11	Bb5	Bd7!
12	Nd5	Qa5+
13	Nc3	Ne5!!
14	de5	Bb5
15	Qd5	a6
16	a4	Rfd8
17	Qc5	Rac8
18	Qb6	Ne3!
19	Qe3	Rd3
20	Qe4	Rdc3
21	bc3	Rc3
22	Rc3	Qc3+
23	Nd2	Qc1
		mate

Now White attacks Black's **B** with two pieces.

15.Qd5

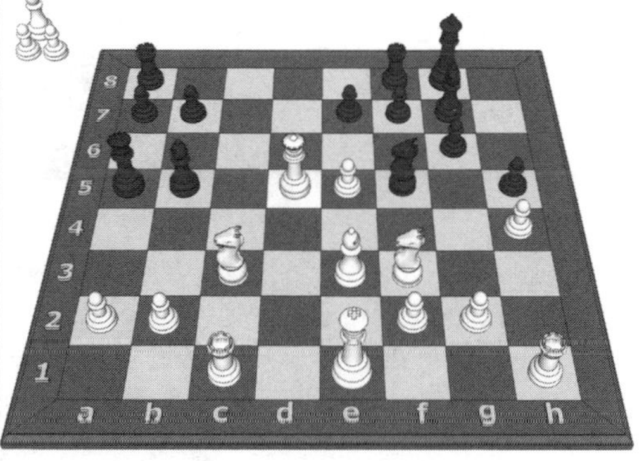

15...a6

Black protects the **B**.

	White	Black
1	e4	c5
2	c3	g6
3	d4	cd4
4	cd4	d5
5	e5	Nc6
6	Nc3	Nh6
7	h4	Nf5
8	Be3	h5
9	Rc1	Bg7
10	Nf3	0-0
11	Bb5	Bd7!
12	Nd5	Qa5+
13	Nc3	Ne5!!
14	de5	Bb5
15	Qd5	a6
16	a4	Rfd8
17	Qc5	Rac8
18	Qb6	Ne3!
19	Qe3	Rd3
20	Qe4	Rdc3
21	bc3	Rc3
22	Rc3	Qc3+
23	Nd2	Qc1
		mate

It looks as if White has won the Black **B**. It is pinned because, if it moves, the Black **Q** is attacked.

16.a4

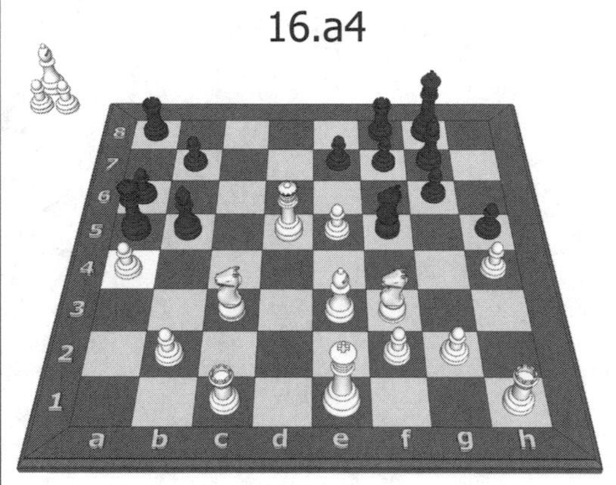

16...Rfd8

Black chases the White **Q** from d5.

	White	Black
1	e4	c5
2	c3	g6
3	d4	cd4
4	cd4	d5
5	e5	Nc6
6	Nc3	Nh6
7	h4	Nf5
8	Be3	h5
9	Rc1	Bg7
10	Nf3	0-0
11	Bb5	Bd7!
12	Nd5	Qa5+
13	Nc3	Ne5!!
14	de5	Bb5
15	Qd5	a6
16	a4	Rfd8
17	Qc5	Rac8
18	Qb6	Ne3!
19	Qe3	Rd3
20	Qe4	Rdc3
21	bc3	Rc3
22	Rc3	Qc3+
23	Nd2	Qc1
		mate

White is still pinning the **B**.

17.Qc5

17...Rac8

Black chases the White **Q** again.

	White	Black
1	e4	c5
2	c3	g6
3	d4	cd4
4	cd4	d5
5	e5	Nc6
6	Nc3	Nh6
7	h4	Nf5
8	Be3	h5
9	Rc1	Bg7
10	Nf3	0-0
11	Bb5	Bd7!
12	Nd5	Qa5+
13	Nc3	Ne5!!
14	de5	Bb5
15	Qd5	a6
16	a4	Rfd8
17	Qc5	Rac8
18	Qb6	Ne3!
19	Qe3	Rd3
20	Qe4	Rdc3
21	bc3	Rc3
22	Rc3	Qc3+
23	Nd2	Qc1
		mate

Looks as if Black will be forced to trade **Q**s.

18.Qb6

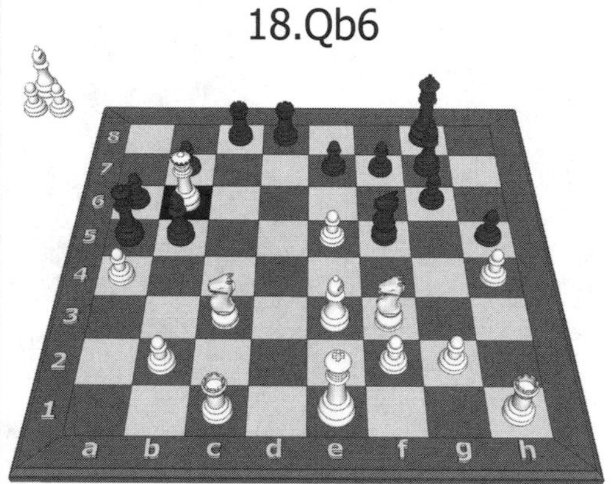

18...Ne3!

Surprise! Black did not take the **Q**. On the next move, White will not be able to move Qxa5, because of Nxg2++.

	White	Black
1	e4	c5
2	c3	g6
3	d4	cd4
4	cd4	d5
5	e5	Nc6
6	Nc3	Nh6
7	h4	Nf5
8	Be3	h5
9	Rc1	Bg7
10	Nf3	0-0
11	Bb5	Bd7!
12	Nd5	Qa5+
13	Nc3	Ne5!!
14	de5	Bb5
15	Qd5	a6
16	a4	Rfd8
17	Qc5	Rac8
18	Qb6	Ne3!
19	Qe3	Rd3
20	Qe4	Rdc3
21	bc3	Rc3
22	Rc3	Qc3+
23	Nd2	Qc1
		mate

The **Q** had to take the **N**.

19.Qe3

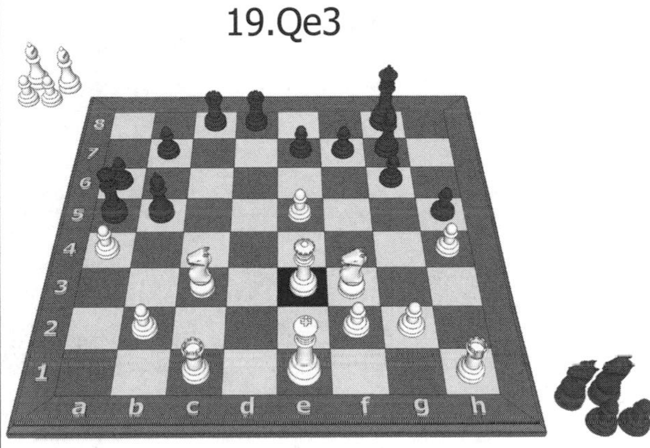

19...Rd3

Black keeps chasing the White **Q**. The **N** on c3 is attacked by three pieces!

	White	Black
1	e4	c5
2	c3	g6
3	d4	cd4
4	cd4	d5
5	e5	Nc6
6	Nc3	Nh6
7	h4	Nf5
8	Be3	h5
9	Rc1	Bg7
10	Nf3	0-0
11	Bb5	Bd7!
12	Nd5	Qa5+
13	Nc3	Ne5!!
14	de5	Bb5
15	Qd5	a6
16	a4	Rfd8
17	Qc5	Rac8
18	Qb6	Ne3!
19	Qe3	Rd3
20	Qe4	Rdc3
21	bc3	Rc3
22	Rc3	Qc3+
23	Nd2	Qc1
		mate

20.Qe4

20...Rdc3

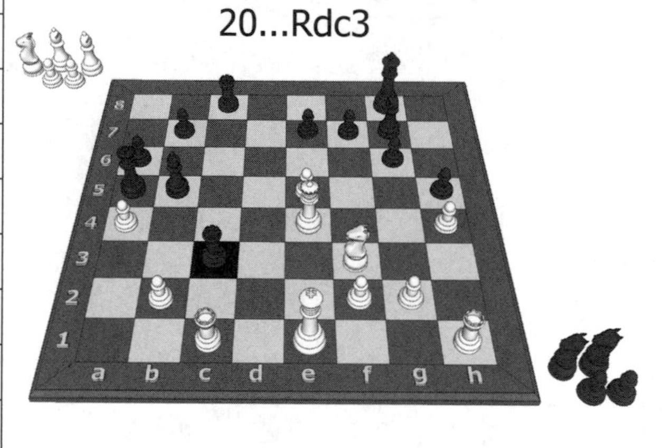

Black sacrifices a **R** for a **N** in order to checkmate White. Can you figure out what is going to happen here?

	White	Black
1	e4	c5
2	c3	g6
3	d4	cd4
4	cd4	d5
5	e5	Nc6
6	Nc3	Nh6
7	h4	Nf5
8	Be3	h5
9	Rc1	Bg7
10	Nf3	0-0
11	Bb5	Bd7!
12	Nd5	Qa5+
13	Nc3	Ne5!!
14	de5	Bb5
15	Qd5	a6
16	a4	Rfd8
17	Qc5	Rac8
18	Qb6	Ne3!
19	Qe3	Rd3
20	Qe4	Rdc3
21	bc3	Rc3
22	Rc3	Qc3+
23	Nd2	Qc1
		mate

21.bc3

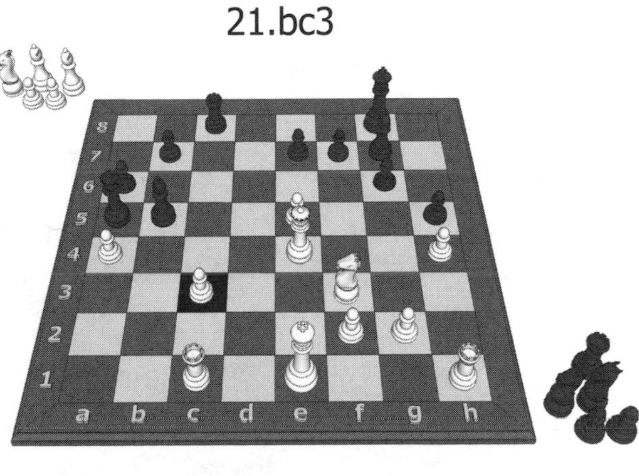

21...Rc3

Now Black is threatening a discovered check. When the **R** moves, the **Q** will be checking the White **K**. We talked about discovered checks earlier.

	White	Black
1	e4	c5
2	c3	g6
3	d4	cd4
4	cd4	d5
5	e5	Nc6
6	Nc3	Nh6
7	h4	Nf5
8	Be3	h5
9	Rc1	Bg7
10	Nf3	0-0
11	Bb5	Bd7!
12	Nd5	Qa5+
13	Nc3	Ne5!!
14	de5	Bb5
15	Qd5	a6
16	a4	Rfd8
17	Qc5	Rac8
18	Qb6	Ne3!
19	Qe3	Rd3
20	Qe4	Rdc3
21	bc3	Rc3
22	Rc3	Qc3+
23	Nd2	Qc1
		mate

White stops the discovered check by taking the **R**.

22.Rc3

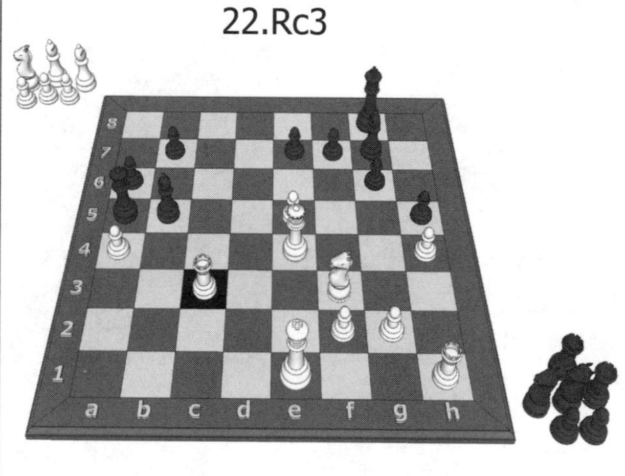

22...Qc3+

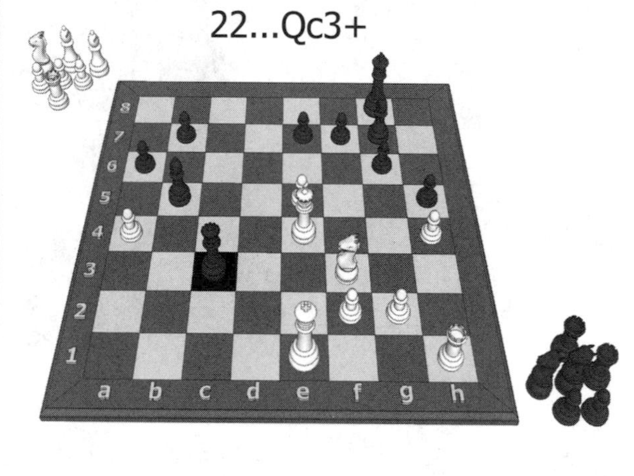

The **Q** checks and is threatening mate.

	White	Black
1	e4	c5
2	c3	g6
3	d4	cd4
4	cd4	d5
5	e5	Nc6
6	Nc3	Nh6
7	h4	Nf5
8	Be3	h5
9	Rc1	Bg7
10	Nf3	0-0
11	Bb5	Bd7!
12	Nd5	Qa5+
13	Nc3	Ne5!!
14	de5	Bb5
15	Qd5	a6
16	a4	Rfd8
17	Qc5	Rac8
18	Qb6	Ne3!
19	Qe3	Rd3
20	Qe4	Rdc3
21	bc3	Rc3
22	Rc3	Qc3
23	Nd2	Qc1
		mate

23.Nd2

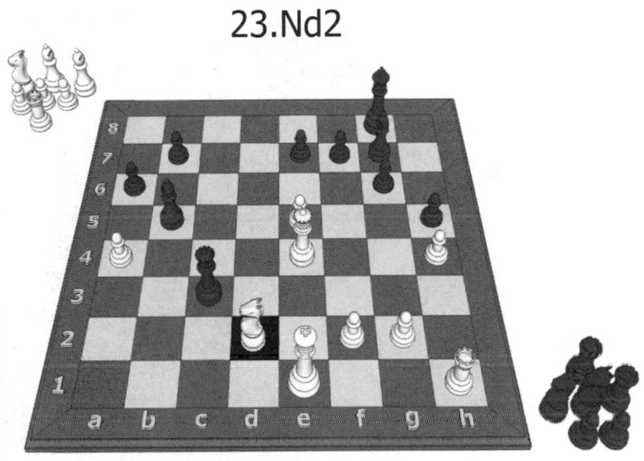

23...Qc1

Checkmate.

Here's another look at the final position.

The good development of Black's pieces has won this game. White is "busted."

V. FINISHING THE JOB

Games do not play themselves. I once had a great game going and I said to myself, "This is so good, it plays itself." Guess what? I lost. The game didn't play itself.

Even if it looks as if you are way out ahead — you're pretty sure of your win — you still need to finish off your opponent. That final checkmate is really important.

When your opponent has only a **K**, you can win with your **K** and a:

- ♔ **Q**
- ♔ **R**
- ♔ 2 **B**s
- ♔ **N** and **B** (difficult)
- ♔ pawn (sometimes)

If you just have a **B** or **N**, there is no mate at all. Even two **N**s can't checkmate. A draw is the best you can do with a **K** and one of these pieces.

This page shows examples of "mates."

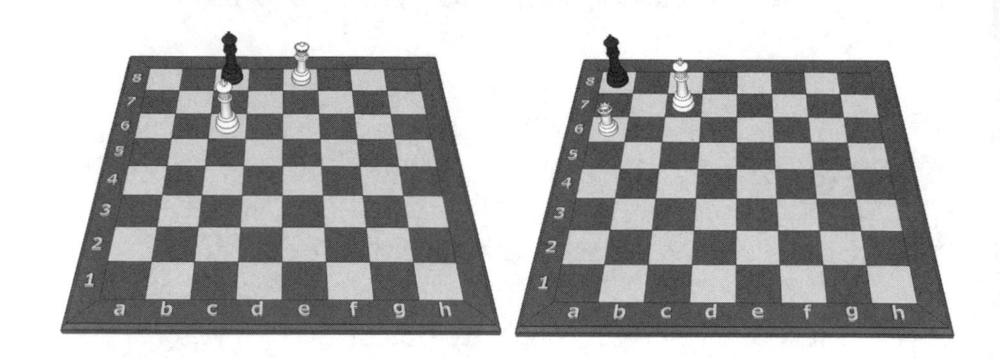

Look for "mates" when you're playing.

Mating with a **K** and **Q**

This is a typical ending, with White to move.

Qe4

Q moves to e4, building a fence.

...Kc8

Black has only one move. C8

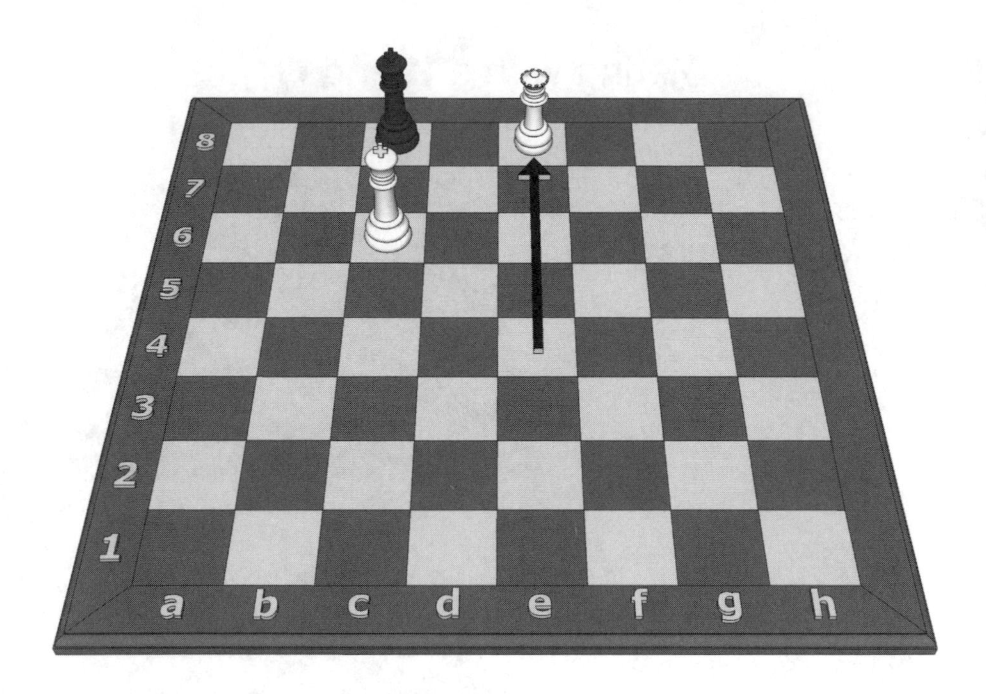

Qe8++

The **Q** has a back rank mate on e8.

Mating with a **K** and **R**

If you have a **K** and **R** against just a **K**, you can always win. You just need to know how. Think of walls or fences, that keep the opponent's **K** in a box. Keep making the box smaller, until the enemy **K** is "squished" with no choices about where to go.

You don't need to keep checking, just keep cutting down the size of the box. The only check in a **K** and **R** ending, should be checkmate!

In this position, it is White to move. The Black **K** has a rectangle smaller than half of the board. You will see the rectangle, or box of the Black **K** get smaller and smaller.

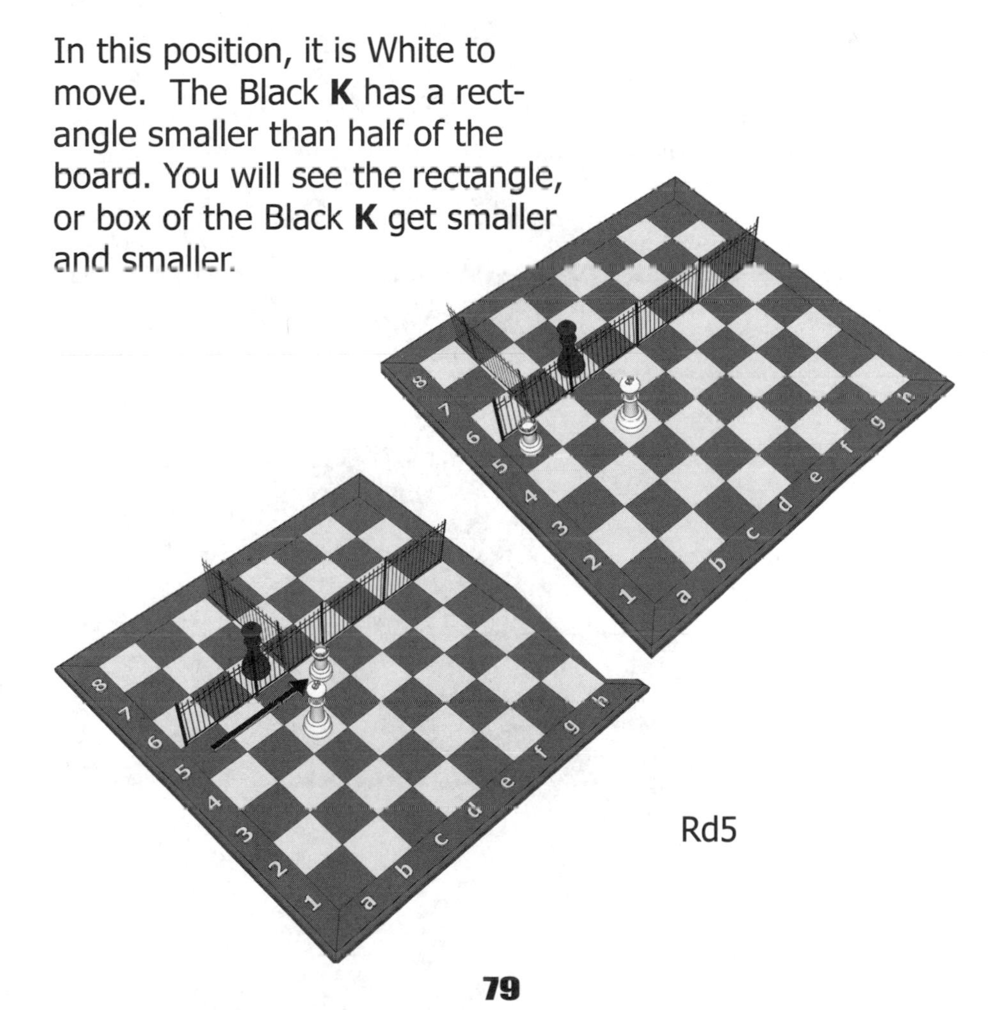

Rd5

... Kb6

No matter what Black does, White will make the box smaller.

Rc5

Pay attention. This is very important.

... Ka6

or a7 or b7, it makes no difference.

Rb5

This is a really good move. That fence is working in both directions.

...Ka7

Kc5

Here comes the cavalry. Remember the **K** is a fighting piece.

...Ka6

Still hoping.

Kc6

...Ka7

Rb6

"Squishing" at its finest.

...Ka8

ouch!

Kc7

...Ka7

Is there a way out?

Rc6

Do you see what's happening?

...Ka8

This is the only move.

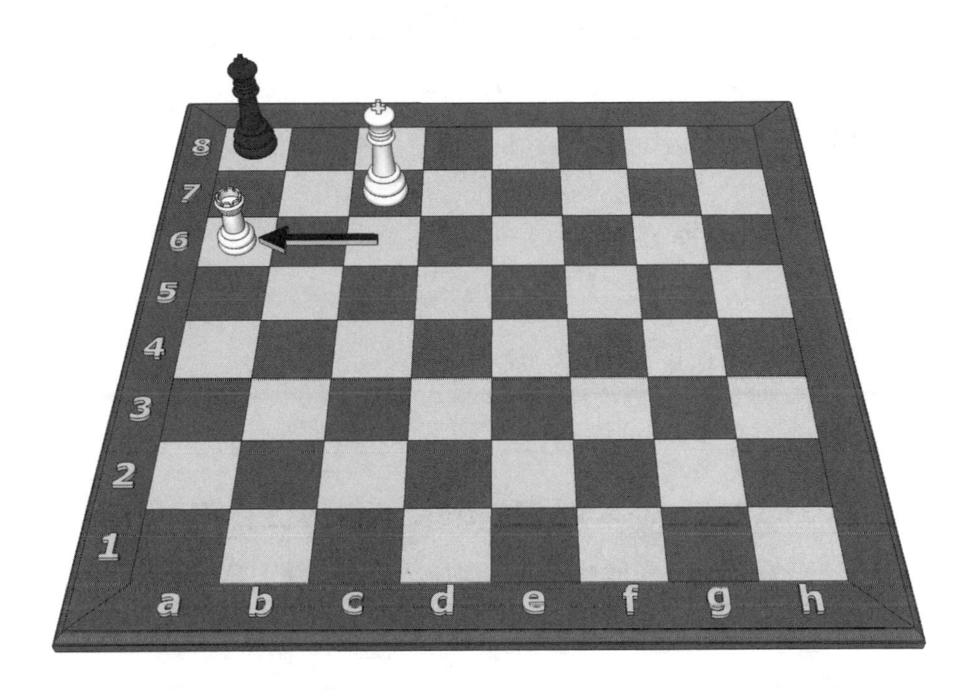

Ra6++

Done – this move says it all. Checkmate!!!!

Mating with a **B** and **B**

No, this is not bed and breakfast – it's bishop and bishop.

With the two **B**s, you can control every color square, on all the diagonals.

In this position, it's White to move.

Bg4

A diagonal fence.

...Ka8

Bh4

This **B** covering the Black squares can go to any square on this diagonal.

...Kb8

Bg3+

...Ka8

Just back and forth.

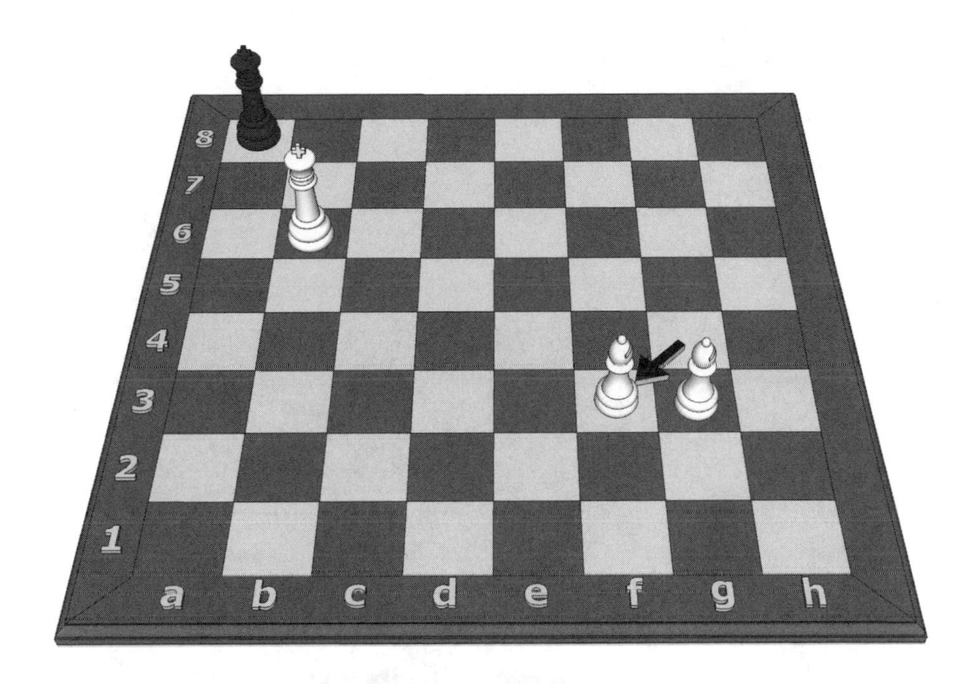

Bf3++

Bang, done, checkmate!!!

Mating with a **N** and **B**

This is an example of a difficult mate with a **N** and a **B**.

It's White's turn to move.

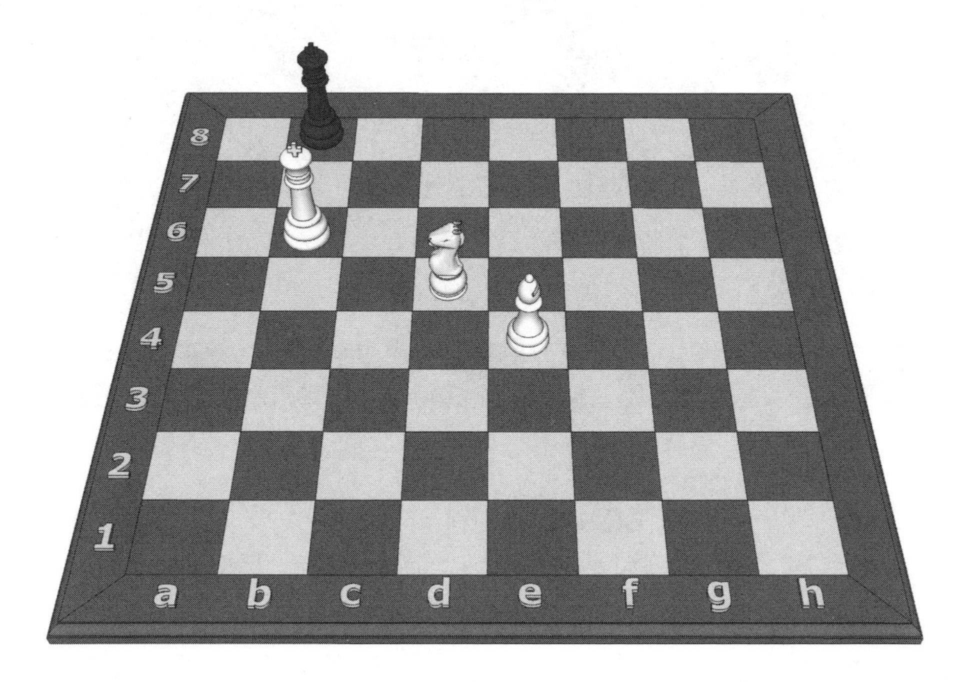

To mate with a **N** and a **B**, force your opponent's **K** to a corner square that is the same color as your **B**.

Bf5

White plays **B** to f5, blocking the **K** from moving out of the corner.

...Ka8

The only legal square for the **K**.

Nb4

Wow, what a move. Can you figure out what's coming?

...Kb8

Again, the only move.

Na6

Check, forcing the **K** back into the corner.

...Ka8

Looks like big trouble for Black.

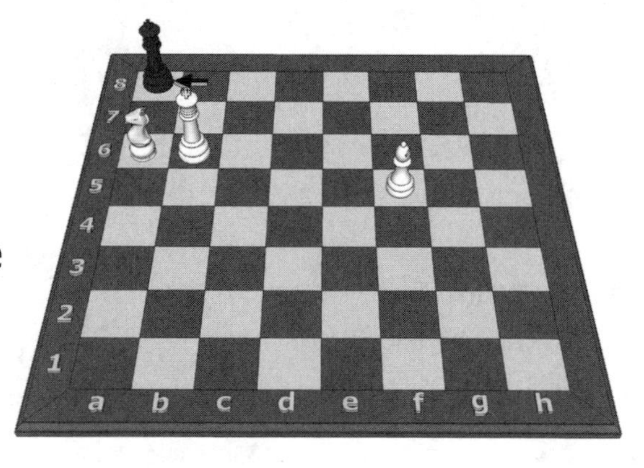

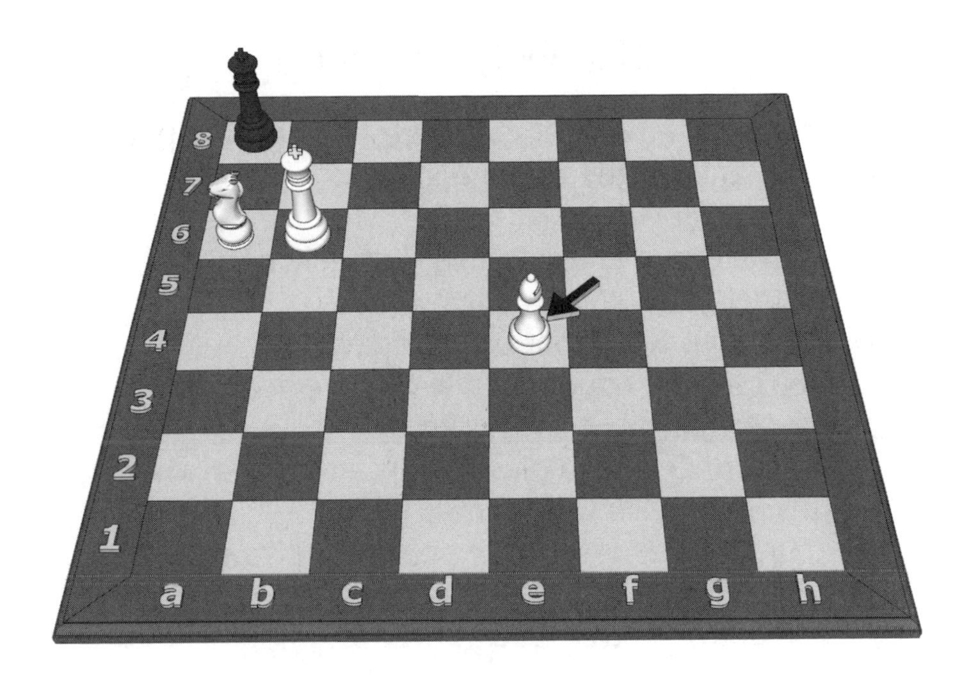

Be4++

That would be checkmate!!!!
A mate like this takes all kinds of care and patience.

Mating with a **K** and **p**

Some things to remember, when you just have a pawn and your **K** against the opponent's **K**.

- ♔ Promote to a **Q** if possible – usually best
- ♔ Protect your pawn with your **K**
- ♔ Keep your **K** in front of your pawn.
- ♔ Don't let the opponent's **K** capture your pawn
- ♔ Be careful not to stalemate
- ♔ An extra **Q** should always win, no matter where the opponent's **K** is located
- ♔ Your chances are best if your pawn is near the center of the board.
- ♔ Rook pawns often end in draws.

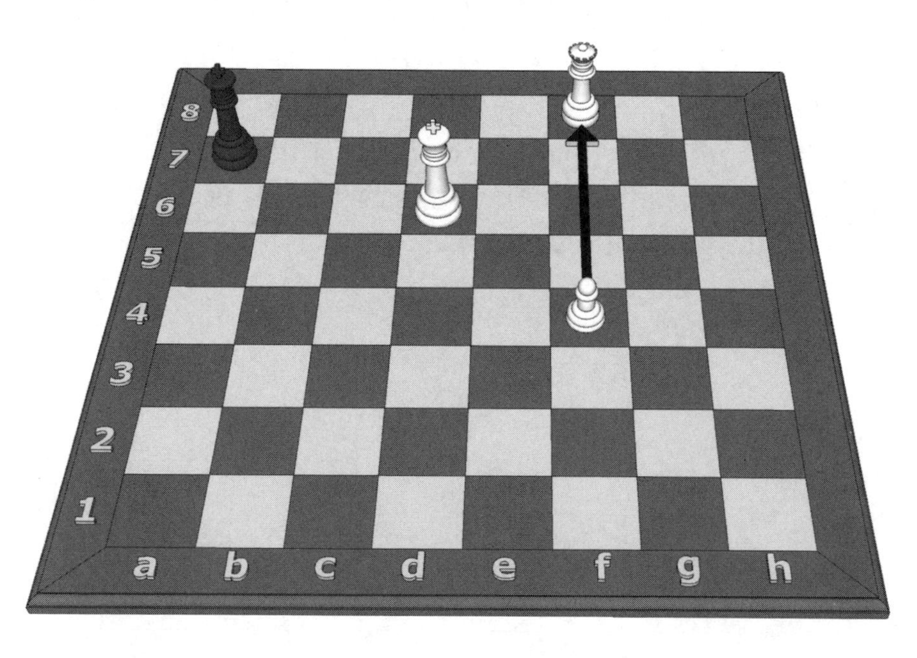

Once you move the White **K** in front of the White pawn, you know you have a win.

The White **K** must move to the side so that the pawn can become a **Q**.

You can see that the White pawn is moving forward. The move checks the Black **K** and pushes it away.

Again, the pawn checks the Black **K** and gets closer to making a new **Q**.

There is no way to stop this pawn.

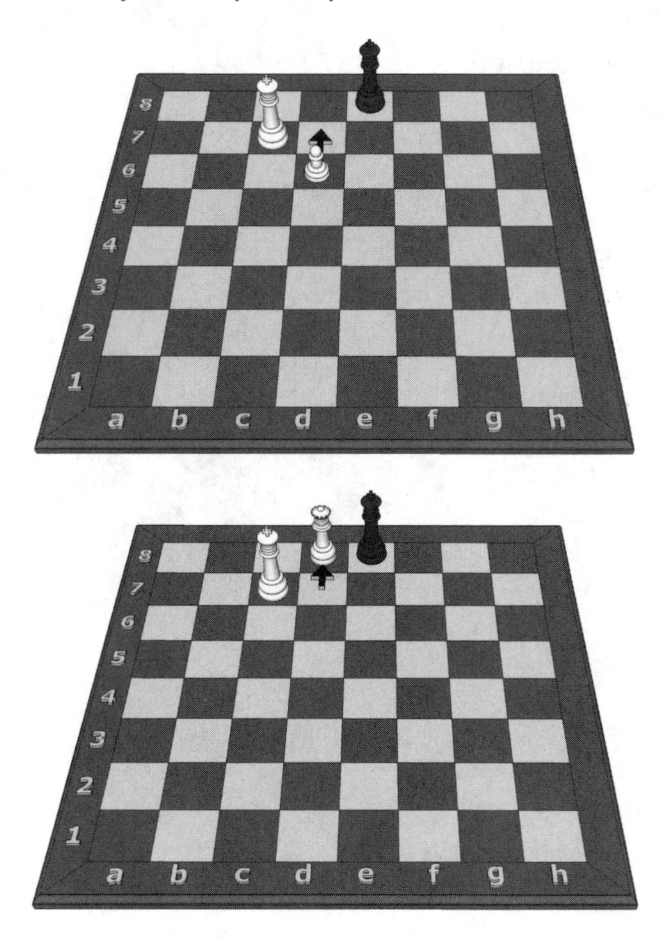

Yes!! Finally a new **Q**! You need to be really patient in this kind of position.

The rest of the game should be easy. Just remember to squish the Black **K**.

Take your time. Be patient.

Don't stalemate.

OOPS – BE CAREFUL

Take a look at the pieces on this board. White seems to be winning. But if it is Black's turn to move the game is a draw. Black has NO legal moves, so it is a stalemate. No one wins. Even though White worked really hard to get this position, it's just a draw. Don't let this happen to you. There are strategies to getting that checkmate — and winning the game.

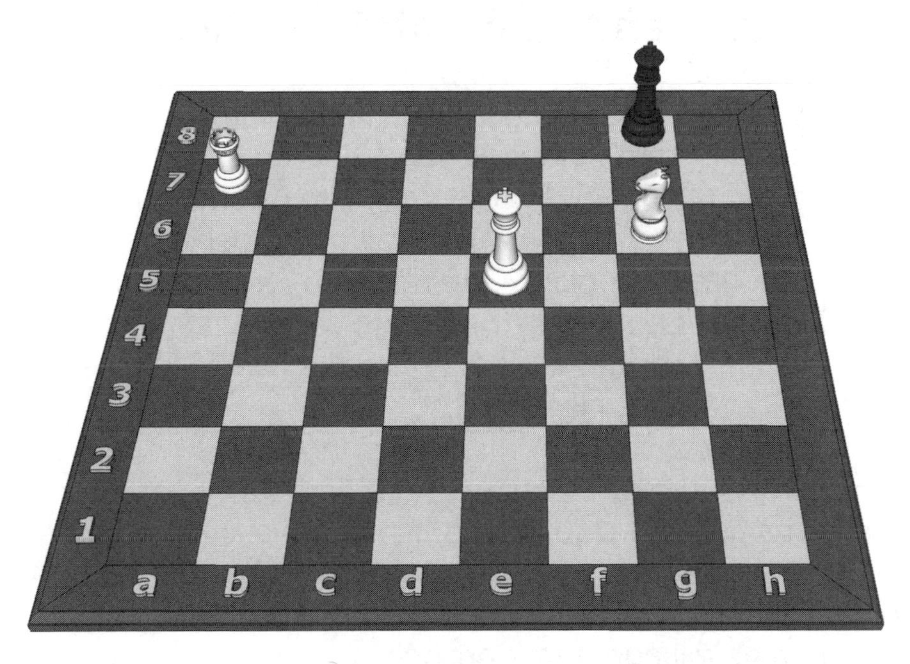

VI. LEARN MORE

Let's look at ways to get better at chess. All the chess players I've met want to get better, but they like to "do their own thing." Some read chess books. Some take lessons from teachers. I just love to play. So, the best way I know to learn chess is to play as much as you can. Try to play with really good players. You may lose every game, but you will learn so much from playing these people. Then, suddenly, one day — surprise! You just may win!

When you do play, really have fun with the game. That way, practicing is terrific instead of a chore.

Join an Organization or Club

Membership in a national organization will put you on the map as a "real" chess player. The United States Chess Federation (USCF), the Canadian Chess Federation, or some such organization will offer special perks. The USCF has a scholastic membership for young players. It includes a monthly magazine with games, quizzes, information, and tournament announcements. Teachers and local clubs are also listed.

Your local club may have a website of its own, that shows games and club results. Many schools have chess clubs or chess classes. They often meet after the school day. If your school doesn't have a club, maybe a teacher or a parent will agree to start one.

Play in Tournaments

Tournaments give players a chance to compete over the board, face to face. After the game, they get to talk about what happened, and go over their game together. Players call this postmortem. It really helps you improve your game. You learn what your mistakes were — and you can fix them!

Use Computer Programs

There are computer programs you can buy to teach you and to help you practice. ChessBase 11 lets you go over games from really good players. Chessmaster 10th Edition, Fritz, or Rybka are good programs to play against, when you start getting strong.

Chess computers that you can hold in your hand are great fun to play with and are especially good on car trips. Chess apps are available to add on to iPods and similar devices.

Take Lessons

Group lessons can give you the basics. They also give you a chance to work on ideas with the teacher or members of the class. You can find chess classes in schools, libraries, community centers, at chess clubs, and sometimes in private homes. These can be great fun.

A teacher can go over your games with you and help you get better. Private lessons with one teacher and one student are very good for serious study of the game. If you live near a big city, it's usually easy to find a chess teacher. Even if you're out in the country, you can often find an expert or master player to work with. Some professional chess teachers will provide long distance instruction. They use e-mail, phones or "Skype" to work with students.

Working with a private teacher can cost you a lot in time and money, so be sure you really want to do that.

Study with a Friend

It's great to have a friend that you can learn with. You can practice together and talk about your moves. This is a lot cheaper than working with a professional player.

Go Over Books and Newspapers

Bookstores carry many chess books at all levels of play — from beginner to master players. You can find inexpensive books on chess or chess games in stores selling used books.

Many local papers run chess columns every week. Check for them in your area. It's cool to play the games over on your own chessboard.

VII. INTERNET IMPACT

The Internet has changed the chess world, more than anything else in recent years. People hardly ever play postal chess, since it's silly to wait for months to play a single game. We are all used to speed – fast communication – more moves, better games, and immediate feedback.

You can use the Internet to play or to learn more about the game of chess. Games are going on every day and all the time — after all, chess is played around the world. When we say "24/7" we mean 24 hours a day, seven days a week. In other words, you can play a real person, in a live game, at your own level of play – any time. Imagine that.

We are providing information about our favorite Internet sites in this section. It's important to remember, that since the Internet is changing all the time, and new web sites are popping up all the time, you can alter your use of the Internet as you learn more.

Use your own favorite search engine and enter words like chess, scholastic, kids, and play. My own favorite search engine is www.google.com.

FREE WEBSITES TO PLAY CHESS

www.Pogo.com/chess
Pogo is a lot of fun. We found it easy to access and to use. Even though it's free, you can win prizes.

www.instantchess.com
Instant chess had no downloads and was easy to play at. This is a strictly "no frills" site, just pure chess.

www.Playfin.com/chess
Playfin had way too many downloads for us, and seemed very complicated.

www.RedHotPawn.com
Far from being "red hot," this site was s-l-o-w. You could take three days for a move, so it could take a year to finish a game. You need to be very patient to play on this site.

www.Chessmaniac.com
This seemed complicated and tough to access.

www.Chesskids.com
Based in England, only for kids.

www.yahoo.com
A popular site with thousands of players.

SCHOLASTIC ORGANIZATIONS

America's Foundation for Chess
Blue Ridge Internet
Chesscoaches.com
Colorado Master Chess, Inc.
Gateway Chess League
Heber Chess Academy for Kids
Kent Scholastic Chess
Nashville Chess Center
New York Scholastic Chess
Rotary Chess Education Initiative
Student Chess
CV Chess
Hawaii/Windward Mall Chess Clubs
National Scholastic Chess Foundation
Nychess.org
NYChessKids
School Chess Association
UCDS Chess

NATIONAL ORGANIZATIONS

United States Chess Federation: **www.uschess.org**
Chess Federation of Canada: **www.chess.ca**

OTHER NOTABLE WEBSITES

Cardoza Publishing: **www.cardozabooks.com** has a full line of chess books — great for learning.

Chess Center: **www.chess-center.com** has junior chess activities.

Canadian Scholastic Chess: **www.chess-math.org**

Chess for Kids: **www.chessforkids.ca** Try this site. It's great.

The International Chess Club (ICC), site **www.Chessclub.com**, costs approximately $60 per year. It is an excellent site, for experienced players, and does offer a free trial.

VIII. CHESS TERMS

Algebraic Notation	System used to write down games, with capital letters for major pieces, lowercase letters for rank and file squares, and symbols for game moves. Used in this book.
Attack	Threatening to win a piece or the game.
Castle	Move a **K** and **R** during one turn. This move can only be used when both the **K** and the **R** are still in their original positions and do not pass through check on the move.
Check	A **K** is threatened.
Checkmate	Also simply "mate." The checked **K** is trapped. Game over.
Closed file	Pawns are in the way. The pieces can't sweep across the board. Opposite of an open file.
Defense	Protecting pieces, squares, and the game. Openings are named "defenses" when Black makes a move to answer an attack by White.
Discovered Check	A piece moves and uncovers another piece, giving check.

Double Check	A check by two different pieces at the same time.
Draw	Both players agree that no one can win. The game is ended.
En passant	When a pawn captures another pawn "in passing," as if the opponent's pawn had only moved one square instead of two on its first move. Also written with the initials "e.p."
Exchange	You take an opponent's piece and he immediately takes your captur ing piece. If you took a **R** for a **N** or a **B**, you've "won the exchange."
File	Each vertical (up and down) column on the chessboard, known by the letters "a" through "h."
Fork	When a piece attacks two piece at once. Usually a **N** move.
Hanging	A piece that has no defense and will be captured is said to be hanging.
Open file	No pawns are in the way. Pieces can move freely from one side of the board to the other. Opposite of closed file.
Opponent	The person you are playing against.

Overworked	When a piece is doing too much in a game. Other pieces are being ignored.
Piece	**N**, **R**, **B**, **Q**, and **K**. The pawn is not counted as a piece, but it can become a **Q** or any other piece if it reaches the end of the board.
Pin	The **K** or some other piece would be placed in danger it this piece is moved – it is "pinned."
Postmortem	Players reviewing moves after the game is over.
Rank	Each horizontal (across) row on the chessboard, known by the numbers "1" through "8."
Rating	For tournament players, the number assigned by the USCF, showing how strong you are, compared to opponents you have played.
Refute	This means saying, "Ha, you thought that was a good move. Guess what, it isn't." You prove your opponent has made a mistake.
Resign	In a hopeless position, give up the game — seeing no way to win. Try not to do this.

Sacrifice	Sometimes simply called, "sac," as in "to sac a piece." You give something up on purpose, to get something even better. If it is accidental, it is not a sacrifice.
Simul	Short for "simultaneous exhibition" when one player plays several boards with different opponents, all at the same time. Usually very strong players try these.
Skewered	A piece is pinned, since it is protecting another piece behind it.
Stalemate	One player whose turn it is, has no legal move. The **K** cannot be "mated" No one wins.
Symbols	Shortcuts for common terms.
Trade	An exchange of like pieces: take one, lose one.
USCF	United States Chess Federation – national association of chess players.

ABOUT THE AUTHORS

Rosalyn B. Katz started playing tournament chess after her son David began to play. She wrote legislation putting chess into New Jersey schools at the second grade level, to encourage "thinking." She has played chess in: Iceland, Canada, France, England, Greece, Israel, Italy, and Switzerland – and all over the United States, when traveling for business. Roz has been writing the cartoon, *Zaria,* for eight years. You can find it in *Chess Life for Kids,* a magazine published by the USCF.

David Lawrence Katz has been playing chess since he was three years old. He won his first trophy in a New York State scholastic tournament when he was six. As a youngster, David played for the "Collins Kids" in: Iceland, Ireland, Israel and the United States. He attained the rank of Life Master in the United States and Master in Canada. Most of his playing is now on the internet... and speed chess for fun. He currently lives in Zurich, Switzerland with his wife Lynel and children: Zaria, Asher and Ella.

GREAT CARDOZA CHESS BOOKS

ADD THESE TO YOUR LIBRARY · ORDER NOW!